AMERICAN

HERITAGE

June 1959 · Volume X, Number 4

In the early years of this century, when a farmer was happy to get his barn painted for nothing—with perhaps a few packages of Mail Pouch thrown in—signs like these were a common feature of the rural landscape. Today advertisers must woo a sophisticated audience whizzing by on expressways that bypass the back country, while Dr. Pierce has given way to multiple vitamins.

AMERICAN HERITAGE

The Magazine of History

PUBLISHER
James Parton

EDITORIAL DIRECTOR
Joseph J. Thorndike, Jr.

EDITOR
Bruce Catton

MANAGING EDITOR
Oliver Jensen

EXECUTIVE EDITOR
Eric Larrabee

ASSOCIATE EDITORS
Richard M. Ketchum
Joan Paterson Mills

ASSISTANT EDITOR
Robert L. Reynolds

EDITORIAL ASSISTANTS
Hilde Heun, Stephen W. Sears
Caroline Backlund, Helen M. Brown
Robert Cowley, Beverly Hill
Naomi S. Weber

ART DIRECTOR
Irwin Glusker

ASSOCIATE ART DIRECTOR: **Murray Belsky**
ASSISTANT: **Trudy Glucksberg**
STAFF PHOTOGRAPHER: **Herbert Loebel**

ADVISORY BOARD
Allan Nevins, *Chairman*
Ray A. Billington   Louis C. Jones
Carl Carmer   Richard P. McCormick
Albert B. Corey   Harry Shaw Newman
Christopher Crittenden   Howard H. Peckham
Marshall B. Davidson   S. K. Stevens
Arthur M. Schlesinger, Sr.

CIRCULATION DIRECTOR
Richard V. Benson

AMERICAN HERITAGE is published every two
months by American Heritage Publishing Co.,
Inc., 551 Fifth Avenue, New York 17, N. Y.
Single Copies: $2.95
Annual Subscriptions: $12.50 in U.S. & Canada
$13.50 elsewhere

An annual Index of AMERICAN HERITAGE is
published every February, priced at $1.00.
AMERICAN HERITAGE is also indexed in
Readers' Guide to Periodical Literature.

AMERICAN HERITAGE will consider but assumes
no responsibility for unsolicited material.

Second class postage paid at New York, N. Y.

Sponsored by
American Association for State & Local History · Society of American Historians

CONTENTS   *June 1959 · Volume X, Number 4*

COVER: Samuel Chester Reid, hero of the battle of Fayal (see page 60), was also
the designer of the present United States flag, which flies behind him in this
portrait by Jarvis. Reid proposed a return to the original thirteen stripes and
the addition of a new star for the admittance of each new state. The portrait
is in the collection of the Minneapolis Institute of Arts. *Back Cover:* These
announcement slides are part of a large collection of early song slides owned
by John W. Ripley of Topeka, Kansas, whose article on illustrated songs begins
on page 50.

Of Raleigh and the First Plantation

The fate of the Virginia Colony rested on the endurance of adventurers, the financing

of London merchants, and the favor of a courtier with his demanding spinster Queen

By A. L. ROWSE

In the marvelous 1580's everything was beginning to ripen together in the heat of the tension between England and Spain. Poetry and the drama that had been so sparse and backward were coming to a head with Sidney and Spenser and Marlowe; the first Elizabethan madrigals appear in the very year the war against Spain begins. And this is the moment when the idea of American colonization takes shape and wing—or, perhaps I should say, takes sail.

The person who had first undertaken to carry out the idea, as to which there had been so much discussion and so many abortive gestures in the direction of it, was Humphrey Gilbert. And from the Crown's patent he was granted in 1578 sprang the ultimate achieve-

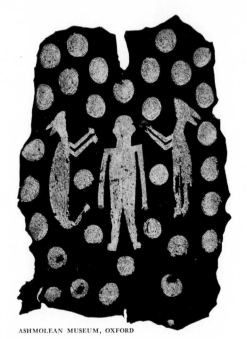

ASHMOLEAN MUSEUM, OXFORD

For all the ruffles and earrings of his court costume, Sir Walter Raleigh (left) embodied qualities the Elizabethan Age admired: style, poetry, good looks, and pride. Men such as he revealed the wonders of the New World to the Old, bringing back tobacco and trophies like the ceremonial cloak of Chief Powhatan (right), made of deerskin decorated with tiny shells, in the figure of a man with an animal on each side.

ment. That patent gave him license for six years "to search, find out and view such remote, heathen and barbarous lands, countries and territories not actually possessed of any Christian prince or people." That was the regular formula, in pursuance of the government's consistent stand on American settlement.

Humphrey Gilbert had been from the days of his youth a personal servant of Queen Elizabeth, from the time when, as Princess, she was in disgrace with her sister Mary. We know little of Gilbert's expedition of 1578, which was secret, very mixed in its make-up—to which some genuinely piratical elements were attached and which turned out a complete failure. It is thought that he was aiming at settlement in Florida. The Queen contributed a ship of her own, the *Falcon:* captain, Walter Raleigh. I cannot help thinking she must have known him, certainly have known of him, long before the traditionally romantic account of her sudden falling for him—to which we have all subscribed.

Walter Raleigh was no new man: he came from a very old family which had already made its place by the time of Henry II.

5

ST. IVES   FALMOUTH

LAND'S END PENZANCE ST. MICHAEL'S MOUNT THE LIZARD   PENDENNIS CASTLE

COURTIER-BACKER: The third Earl of Southampton was a supporter of the Virginia Company and for a time its treasurer. History knows him best as the generous patron of Shakespeare. As a young man he played a part in the Earl of Essex's conspiracy and narrowly escaped with his life.

POET-BACKER: England had Sir Philip Sidney's heart, and he hers, to paraphrase him. The soldier who died so young, the author of famous poems to "Stella," took an eager interest in the enterprises of Frobisher, Drake, and Raleigh. Only Elizabeth's own order kept him from joining Drake against the Spaniards in 1585. Next year, at only 32, he fell fighting in Holland.

This delicately drawn map of the south coast of England in the time of Henry VIII, marked with notices to mariners and as accurate as it is decorative, is in the British Museum and has never been reproduced in its entirety. Above are three sections of it covering the coast of Cornwall and Devon, from Land's End (far left) to Exmouth, showing the harbors from which nearly all the West Country voyages to America set sail. The pivot is Plymouth Sound, shown with St. Nicholas' Island lying off the Hoe—after the Armada it became known as

But by Raleigh's time the family had lost most of its property and become rather impoverished—a most humiliating and irritating situation, especially for an ambitious young man, to feel that you are somebody and haven't a bean. Something of this irritation may be seen all through Raleigh's career: he was always a man in a hurry, conscious of his gifts and abilities, yet always made to wait on circumstances—and maddened by frustration. And there *was* a yellow streak in Raleigh too—he was a great liar—a rift in him by which perhaps came the genius, for men have the qualities of their defects. There is no doubt of the genius; he bore all the stigmata of it.

Raleigh's mother was by birth a Champernowne, and widow of a Gilbert, so that these Gilberts—John, Humphrey, Adrian—were half brothers of Walter and Carew Raleigh. The Gilberts were brought up at Greenway on the Dart, the family seat being Compton Castle, that delightful rose-red H-shaped house of

Drake's Island. At Cattewater began the voyages of Hawkins and Drake, and here Drake returned from his voyage round the world. From here too departed the New England ventures of Sir Ferdinando Gorges; and hence set out the Mayflower. *Near the estuary of the Dart, with its port of Dartmouth, lived the Gilberts. From this haven Sir Humphrey Gilbert made sail on his Newfoundland voyage, and John Davis, in his search for the Northwest Passage. Near Exmouth, Sir Walter Raleigh was born.*

SAILOR-BACKER: Sir Humphrey Gilbert, well-born, well-educated (Eton and Oxford) half brother of Raleigh, was a long-time advocate of the Northwest Passage, sailed from Plymouth in 1583 to make a "Western Planting" in America. The Queen had complained that Gilbert was "of not good hap by sea," and sure enough he was lost during the voyage back to England.

BISHOP-BACKER: Even the cloth ventured money in the new lands. Among the investors was the Archbishop of Canterbury, George Abbot, the first Oxford man to become Archbishop since the Reformation. A Surrey clothworker's son, he founded a hospital in his native town of Guildford.

the fourteenth century, near Torquay, of which the roofless hall has been restored by Commander Walter Raleigh Gilbert in recent years. Humphrey Gilbert was some fifteen years older than Raleigh, and to him the young Walter owed his lead in sea enterprises and ideas of American colonization. Where Gilbert led—at Oxford, in France and Ireland, at sea, over America—Raleigh followed. They had strong family characteristics in common: they were impulsive and intemperate, impatient of any opposition (they had all the more to put up with). They were not very nice men, but they had fascination and they were well educated. They were men of ideas—indeed with them ideas went to their head—and they had great imagination: they were projectors.

Gilbert's failure and, no doubt, the Queen's intimate knowledge of his defects of temperament made her reluctant to support his last and most elaborate project, which has been described as branching out into "a maze of individual and corporate enterprises for the conquest and settlement of North America. . . ." She held Gilbert to be "a man noted of not good hap by sea"; however, against her better judgment, she relented and gave him permission to go. Before he left, with characteristic graciousness, she sent him by Walter Raleigh—now in the first flush of favor—her good wishes, with a jewel for token, "an anchor guided by a Lady." She asked him to leave his portrait with Raleigh for her; she did not invest in the voyage. Gilbert went, took possession of Newfoundland, lost his flagship with all his stores, and was drowned in the barque *Squirrel* on the way home.

Walter Raleigh was the heir to Gilbert's colonizing projects, the man who carried them into execution. But it was entirely his favor with the Queen that gave him the resources to put his plans into operation: the prestige and opportunities of his position, the support and service he could now command, the gifts of lands and licenses, the cash. Notice that the Queen's favor was not given for noth-

ing: there was an implied contract of service. It was her way of attaching men of ability to the service of the state, and from the men she delighted to favor, the state got good service. In all Raleigh's efforts for Virginia she was behind him: she backed him, she provided his resources. In addition, she made her own direct contribution.

In preparation for Raleigh's first Virginia colony, the geographer Richard Hakluyt wrote his *Discourse of Western Planting:* "Certain Reasons to induce her Majesty and the state to take in hand the western voyage and the planting therein." It was an extremely able state paper, unique in that age in putting forth a complete argument for colonial expansion, on every ground—economic, political, strategic, religious—with a plan for its execution and a program of settlement. Raleigh got Hakluyt an audience with the Queen, to whom he presented it on his knees. No doubt she read it: it was meant for her eyes, and was never printed until our own time. But she was not persuaded.

The argument was that only the resources of the state could accomplish the colonization of America.

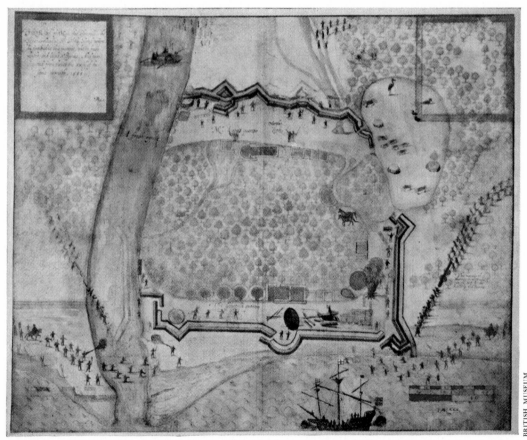

Since the Queen could not spare Raleigh, command of the first Virginia colony went to his cousin, Sir Richard Grenville, who built the fort on St. John's Island in the West Indies (shown in John White's map, above) before he landed in Virginia in 1585. The Tyger *is at anchor, Grenville's quarters are at center, while Grenville himself, on horseback, is across the river (left).*

Sir Richard Grenville, sea captain, commander of the first English colony to get a secure foothold on American shores.

There was something in that: so many were to fail, fall by the wayside, having ventured everything and lost; the sacrifices in wealth and manpower, in suffering, privation, and human life, were immense and terrible. But—a state enterprise? In that age everyone plundered the government and every governmental undertaking. The Queen knew that better than anyone. Had she not often had occasion to utter a *cri de coeur* against the "insatiable cupidity of men"? Then, too, a state enterprise meant a head-on collision with Spain, a frontal challenge from which no retreat was possible. Failure would mean a total loss of prestige to the state. There can be no doubt that the Queen was right to put it aside, and there it remained unknown till our day.

But this did not mean that she was not as anxious as anyone that colonization should succeed. Ultimately it did, under a characteristically mixed English form of enterprise, with private and public elements, and the Crown making a quasi-official contribution. The colonizing Queen made a good profit on her investments, and not least important, she contributed the symbolic name to Virginia.

Everything with this politic woman meant something. The permission to use the name was not mere coquettishness, not only the suggestion of romance which, genuine enough in that day, it has come chiefly to signify for us. It was, like everything with her, an intensely personal act, calling attention to an aspect of her personality which, if not unique in a ruler, was an unforgettable element in her fame. But it was also politics, a characteristically ambivalent notice to the world that she personally was involved as well as the Crown of England; her good name pledged. It was therefore an unmistakable underlining of her claim, which could not chivalrously be disregarded, a warning to others to keep off.

The name caught on at once—it evidently had life in it—with the poets no less than the seamen, the politicians, and merchants. In these same eighties, while Ralph Lane was writing from Virginia to her Secretary Walsingham of the "assurance of her Majesty's greatness hereby to grow by the addition of such a kingdom as this is to the rest of her dominions," Raleigh's friend Edmund Spenser was writing:

Or fruitfullest Virginia who did ever view?

In April, 1584, Raleigh dispatched two barques, under Captains Philip Amadas and Arthur Barlow, to reconnoiter a site for a colony in the southern section of the North American coast. They went out by the southern route via the Canaries and West Indies and then up to Cape Hatteras to the low-lying coast of what is now North Carolina, where among the shoals and lagoons they pitched on an island which they considered a promising site. The advantages of an island for purposes of defense are obvious, and the fact that it was situated among those sounds, with about the most difficult navigation in the world, afforded it some protection from Spanish attentions. Amadas and Barlow brought back a lyrical account of the country and its commodities, and also two lusty young Indians of standing, Wanchese and

The largest venture yet, eight sail commanded by Sir George Somers (right), set out in 1609. But the flagship was wrecked in Bermuda (above), suggesting Shakespeare's The Tempest.

10

Behind the scenes in London two rival figures were Sir Edwin Sandys (left), professional politician and for a time treasurer of the Virginia Company;

and capable Sir Thomas Smythe, the first governor of the East India Company and one of the most influential merchants engaged in colonial affairs.

Manteo, the first of whom was to belie these sanguine hopes, the second to remain ever faithful to the English. In that, the pattern of so much in the subsequent story of relations between the races was foreshadowed early.

That same year, while they were away, Raleigh's first big colonial effort was taking shape. In December the bill confirming his letters patent was before Parliament, and on second reading was handed over to a committee with an interesting membership. There were the Queen's Vice-Chamberlain, Sir Christopher Hatton; her principal Secretary, Sir Francis Walsingham; Sir Philip Sidney, Sir Francis Drake, Sir Richard Grenville, Sir William Courtenay, Sir William Mohun, and other West Country members specially interested in these matters. Upon third reading, the bill, "after many arguments and a proviso added unto it, passed." No one has observed that this long proviso was directed against the expedition undertaking hostilities by sea or land; no doubt that was due to Lord Burghley's influence, and represented a concession to his point of view. By the time the little fleet set sail, open war with Spain made the proviso out of date—and privateering on the way home more than paid the expenses.

The Queen at this time not being able to part with Raleigh, the command was handed over to his cousin. Sir Richard Grenville. There are things to be said against Grenville, all (and rather more than all) said by his second-in-command, Ralph Lane, a cousin of

Sir Edward Dyer and an equerry to the Queen—but he did the job. He made a successful cruise to the West Indies, where he took on board horses and kine to stock the colony, and plants, including sugar, to plant. At the end of June he landed the colony on Roanoke Island. He remained there for a month exploring and prospecting, and then hovered off Cape Hatteras for another month—watching out for what he could find, I suppose—at the end of which he set sail for England. On September 18 "the general came with the prize to Plymouth and was courteously received by divers of his worshipful friends."

That expedition to plant the first colony in America had an interesting membership. In addition to Grenville and Ralph Lane, there was the brilliant young navigator Thomas Cavendish from Suffolk, the second Englishman to make a successful voyage round the world. Also upon it were Thomas Hariot—the first scientist in the country—and John White, one of its best draftsmen, cartographer and illustrator of the expedition. Most of the leading spirits were West Country relations or neighbors of Grenville and Raleigh: one observes among the names an Arundell, a Stukeley, a Prideaux, a Bonython, a Kendall and, I am glad to say, Anthony Rouse, a friend of Drake.

Left to himself in command, Lane responded with a violent outburst against Grenville, full of the usual Elizabethan persecution mania and complaining of the unruliness of "the wild men of mine own nation,"

11

let alone living among savages. It is clear that what they needed was a Grenville to keep them in order; it is also clear that the Queen's equerry was not the type, and indeed he does not appear again in colonial enterprises.

It is not my purpose to tell once more the story of this first English colony in America, what happened to the hundred or so men—that became the usual number dispatched in these early efforts at settlement—upon Roanoke Island during the year almost that they remained there. But in fact, everything goes back to that first colony, to the colonial experience they gathered there, the knowledge as to the physical conditions, the flora and fauna, the products of the soil—above all, what they learned about Indian life, native ways and food, the difficulties of relations with the Indians.

The fundamental lesson that early colonists failed to learn was the absolute necessity of getting down to cultivate the soil. But we must remember to what an extent they consisted of rag, tag, and bobtail who would not learn anything, idle and listless, recalcitrant to all discipline. (Here is where the grand advantage of the Puritans came in, when it came to their turn, in moral fiber and self-discipline.) The dependence of the early colonists on the Indians for food supplies naturally created acute troubles between them, for there was not enough to go round. Their relations, the characters of the Indian chiefs, the troubles between the natives and the newcomers, provide the chief interest of the story.

Raleigh's promised supply ship was late in getting to sea; meanwhile, Grenville was fitting out a larger expedition upon the North Devon coast. The Roanoke colonists were ready to remain and wait, when their nerve was suddenly broken by one of those tornadoes that that coast enjoys—and the prime defect of Roanoke was that it had no satisfactory harbor. When in June, 1586, Drake arrived off the coast with a powerful fleet from his West Indian expedition, on which he had wrought so much destruction, he offered to take the colonists back with him, and on a sudden impulse they decided to accept. If Lane had been a stronger man, he would have stuck it out. . . . And

TEXT CONTINUED ON PAGE 105
ILLUSTRATIONS CONTINUED ON FOLLOWING PAGES

At right, a map of the American coast from Florida to the Chesapeake by John White (see next page) shows with red dots the points in "La Virgenia Pars" where English settlers landed. Raleigh's coat of arms in bright scarlet—and a sea filled with ships, flying fish, and disporting dolphin—decorate the geography, remarkably accurate for the time.

John White's America

The first artist to paint American Indians, American flora and fauna, was a remarkable draftsman, John White, first of the English water-colorists to come over, with Raleigh's first colony (under Grenville); later he returned as governor with a colony of his own. Seventy-five of White's spirited and detailed water colors survive, of which sixty-three were made while he was at Roanoke. A number, like the drawing of a religious dance at right, were borrowed by the publisher Theodore de Bry and taken to Frankfurt, where engravings were made from them to illustrate the Virginia volume in a lengthy series called Grands et petits voyages (1590–1634). White's originals, in which the Indians are far more realistically depicted than by de Bry, disappeared from view for nearly two centuries, but eventually they were rediscovered and after a checkered history now repose in the British Museum. White was fascinated not only by the aborigines and their behavior but by tropical fish, the flamingo and the tortoise (below), and a baby crocodile—the "allagatto" at lower right. His fifth and last voyage to Virginia was a complete failure. "Yet, seeing that it was not my first unsuccessful voyage," he wrote to Richard Hakluyt, "I must rest content. And without having obtained my wishes, I leave off attempting that in which I would to God my wealth could support my will."

Allagatto. This being but one moneth old was 3. foote
4. ynches in length . and lyue in water.

15

16

Over this richly colored tablecloth at Somerset House in London in 1604, the Spanish commissioners (left) met with the English (right) to end their long war, a triumph for Robert Cecil, Lord Burghley's son, who thus achieved the peace his father had wanted. As to America, the treaty said nothing—which meant, in effect, that English colonization would continue.

The English (left to right, in this painting attributed to Gheeraerts) are Thomas Sack-ville, Earl of Dorset and co-author of the first English tragedy, Gorboduc; *Charles How-ard, Earl of Nottingham and Lord High Admiral against the Armada; Charles Blount, Earl of Devonshire; Henry Howard, Earl of Northampton; and Robert Cecil, later Earl of Salisbury.*

17

THE FALL OF RALEIGH

SIMON WINGFIELD DIGBY, M.P.; COURTESY *Life*

Elizabethan court life centered on the Queen, as when one of her maids of honor was being married (above). The scene, painted by Marcus Gheeraerts the Younger, shows Elizabeth on the way to Blackfriars on June 16, 1600. The bride, Anne Russell, is at right; the bridegroom's father, the Earl of Worcester, a Knight of the Garter, is at center in his pink doublet; but the figure of the Queen in her palanquin, borne by six knights, dominates the occasion. For those who sought her support, she was a jealous mistress. Hot-blooded men like Raleigh had to pay constant suit to their unmarried sovereign, a woman as willful as they were, and walk a narrow path, never too close, never too far. Sometimes they slipped.

Raleigh fell decisively from favor in 1592, a result of his affair with Elizabeth Throckmorton (right), another of the royal maids of honor, whom he was compelled to marry. Raleigh was devoted to her until the end. When "the wisest fool in Christendom," James I (above), became king, Raleigh's warlike anti-Spanish policies were doomed, and in 1618 he was beheaded (below). His last poem (below right) was written the evening before he died.

Even such is time, that takes in trust
Our youth, our joys, our all we have,
And pays us but with age and dust;
Who in the dark and silent grave,
When we have wandered all our ways,
Shuts up the story of our days.
But from this earth, this grave, this dust,
My God shall raise me up, I trust!

Part hero, part rogue, Boston's Jim Curley triumphed over the

Brahmins in his heyday, but became in the end a figure of pity

The Last
of the Bosses

By FRANCIS RUSSELL

For the first half of this century and beyond, James Michael Curley was the most flamboyant and durable figure on Boston's political scene. Mayor off and on for a total of sixteen years, he spent four terms in Congress and two in jail, and for two depression years he was governor of Massachusetts. At his death he lay in state for two days in the State House Hall of Flags, the fourth person in the history of the Commonwealth to be so honored. His seventeen-room neo-Georgian mansion on Jamaicaway with shamrocks cut in its shutters was both a landmark of the rise of the immigrant Irish and a nose-thumbing in the direction of Yankee Beacon Hill. He has been hated by Proper Bostonians with a proper and ultimate hatred and held in mindless affection by the slums. Alternately his Irish-American political associates embraced and knifed him. Counted out a score of times, he always bounced back. On several occasions, and long before his death, he received the last rites of the Catholic Church.

His political career began midway between the famine in Ireland and the present. In 1847, that *annus mirabilis,* came the first wave of mass immigration to America. Because the Cunard Line terminus was then at Boston, the wretched Irish landed there. Illiterate, sunk in their defeat, they came like cattle. Five per

Curley, left, joining a Stevenson demonstration at the 1952 Democratic convention, was the epitome of the big-city boss: outgoing, garrulous, a master at political maneuver.

cent of them died on the "coffin ships" on the way over. Transported from their primitive earthbound existence, they were forced to take whatever work they could find at hand, usually in a glutted market—or else starve. Sometimes they did starve in their reeking Paddyvilles and Mick Alleys, where they lived packed closely together in the first urban mass slums of America.

They were the butt of the social pyramid, the unfailing source of exploitable labor: ditchdiggers, stevedores, hod carriers, stableboys. Boston was the center of cheap labor for the country. Construction bosses all over America sent there for fresh supplies of Irish workers. The Paddies went as contract laborers in coaches with sealed doors, the curtains nailed across the windows. Along the Erie Canal and the new railroad lines they died like flies. Jeremiah O'Donovan-Rossa wrote of "the wreck and ruin that came upon the Irish race in this foreign land."

These unassimilable foreigners with their uncouth solidarity more than doubled the population of static Boston, turning it from a coherent and comprehensive town to an incoherent and incomprehensible metropolis. Dismayed, the Old Yankees retreated into themselves, originating the so-called Boston Brahminism as a kind of defense. The term Brahmin, which Dr. Oliver Wendell Holmes had given them quite by accident, they took for self-assurance, and the name stuck, coming to mean not Dr. Holmes's disinterested bread-and-water asceticism of the mind

Left: With his contemporary, New York's dapper, song-writing Jimmy Walker, Curley arrived in Detroit in June, 1932, for a Mayors' Conference. Right: Curley toured Massachusetts with F. D. R. during the 1932 presidential campaign.

Above: In 1935 Governor Curley shook hands with comedian Al Schacht at Boston's Fenway Park. Below: Some years later, mayor again, he rode in a St. Patrick's Day parade. Under the beret is parade marshal Edward "Knocko" McCormack.

but a class-conscious membership in the Yankee State Street financial oligarchy. The Irish were untouchables. Mayor Theodore Lyman called them "a race that will never be infused with our own, but on the contrary will always remain distinct and hostile."

Somewhat over a hundred years later we find Senator John Kennedy—indistinguishable in manner and appearance from his Yankee counterparts, author of *Profiles in Courage,* Pulitzer Prize winner, a member of the Harvard Board of Overseers—a possible presidential candidate. It is interesting sociologically that this upright young man is the grandson of Curley's predecessor as mayor, John F. Fitzgerald—known as "Honey Fitz" for his rendering of "Sweet Adeline" at political rallies.

James M. Curley was a transition figure, a symbol of the emergence of the famine Irish from their proletarian status to political dominance. It is the recurring phenomenon of one class replacing another. In 1776 the Boston merchant oligarchy succeeded the Tory squirearchy by revolution. It in turn, if more slowly and by attrition, was superseded by the Celts. Curley's career is a symbol of this process.

His father, Michael, came to Boston from Galway in 1865 at the age of fourteen. Sarah Clancy, his mother, arrived that same year—a meager-boned Connemara girl of the type Dr. Gogarty called Firbolg. She was twelve years old and worked first as a maid on Beacon Hill. Michael Curley became a hod carrier at ten cents an hour by the grace of Patrick "Pea-Jacket" Maguire, boss of Ward 17, where Galway men clustered. Michael Curley was good-looking in a stumpy, plodding, impassive way, strong, and as he grew older, bearded. At 21 he married Sarah and took her to a tiny flat in one of the rotting three-deckers off Northampton Street. Along Roxbury Neck there were hundreds of those fetid wooden tenements that had been run up by jerry-builders for the shanty Irish. Beyond Northampton Street lay the North Bay, and at low tide the marsh gas sifting in across the mud mixed with the sour permanent stench of the Southampton Street dump. It was said that in Ward 17 children came into the world with clenched fists. In that Roxbury flat James Michael Curley, the second son, was born in 1874.

The boy's horizon was the water-front slum. By the time he was five he ran with an urchin gang, pilfering, dodging the cops, wandering along the edge of the Roxbury flats while the herring gulls wheeled overhead, scaling stones at the wharf rats that scuttled across the dumps, selling old whiskey bottles they found there to Jakie the Junkie. Daily they would see the angular masts and spars of the cargo schooners coming up the Fort Hill channel from far-off places like Maine or Nova Scotia. In the summer they played about the old Roxbury canal or swam in the murky South Bay. Evenings as they lay in bed they could hear the bullfrogs croaking from the marshes. Sometimes, very rarely, in the heat-struck weather they wandered outside the ward. Only a little over a mile to the north was the newly filled area of the Back Bay with its wide avenues and brownstone-front town houses. To tenement boys these opulent mansions with their turrets and gablings seemed like castles.

By the time Jim reached grammar school he was peddling papers. Afternoons he worked as a bundle and delivery boy at the Washington Market. When he was ten his father died. Mike Curley had always been proud of his own strength. One of the workmen challenged him to lift a 400-pound edgestone onto a wagon. He managed to raise it but then collapsed. Three days later he was dead.

The Curleys were then living in an alley tenement in Fellows Court. Pea-Jacket's point of view was limited—no votes, no help. And there was no help for the Curleys.

Sarah kept the family together by scrubbing floors in a downtown office building. Jim and his brother John, two years older, wrapped bundles and served customers at the Washington Market in their free time until the end of grammar school—their last schooling. At twelve, Jim was working in Gale's drugstore an hour and a half before he went to school, and from half past four until eleven after school.

Reared in poverty, alienated from any sense of community, young Jim Curley formed his hard, unwavering, egocentric determination to succeed. Success, the road up from the Fellows Court flat to the imagined great house, was through politics. He knew that when he was still in short trousers. There was no other road for an Irish slum boy. Politics, then, was a game he would take as he found it, not to change the game or reform it, but to win. In the harshness of his own few years he grasped instinctively Boss Martin Lomasney's Neoplatonic axiom that politically speaking the mass of people are interested mainly in food, clothing, and shelter. For these they would barter their votes.

At fifteen, after a series of small jobs, he settled for the next eight years as a deliveryman driving a wagon for C. S. Johnson, Grocers. He was strong like his father, wily and wiry, and except for his somewhat vulpine nose, handsome. He had a resonant voice and soon learned to modify the harshness of his gutter speech. From time to time he would drop in at Curran's livery stable, where the wardheelers gathered, or at One-Armed Peter Whalen's tobacco store, the political hangout of the district.

Free on bail after his 1946 mail fraud conviction, Mayor Curley was welcomed back to Boston (above) by 5,000 admirers. In June, 1947 (below), after long delays and futile legal appeals, he surrendered to begin serving his term.

Curley's five months in jail robbed him of much of his fighting spirit. Then, in 1949, he was defeated for the mayoralty by John B. Hynes, an honest administrator whom Curley had sneered at as "a little city clerk." Outwardly Curley made light of his defeat, but at 74 he knew that he was finished. In 1950 came the crowning blow: his daughter Mary and his son Leo died on the same day, and Curley (right) looked old, shaken, sunk in his grief.

Meanwhile, he enrolled two nights a week at the Boston Evening High School. In the public library he read Dickens and Thackeray and Shakespeare, and the Boston *Transcript*. He taught Sunday school, ushered and passed the plate at St. Philip's on Harrison Avenue, and joined the Ancient Order of Hibernians. He became chairman of committees for picnics, outings, minstrel shows, and church supper dances. For his straight purpose, games and girls and conviviality had no meaning. Time was too short, life too dear.

He knew the families on his grocery route as if they were his own family; he talked with people—after church, at the Hibernians, at Whalen's, on committees. Always he was obliging and always available. By the time he reached his majority he showed the indefinable air of future success that a sixth-sense "pol" like Whalen could spot at once. In 1898 One-Armed Peter tipped him to run for the Boston Common Council against Pea-Jacket's organization, and staked him to his first contribution. Curley won by several hundred votes, but by the time Pea-Jacket's henchmen had finished with the ballot boxes, he found himself counted out. The next year, organizing his own strong-arms and after weeks of pre-election gang fights and corner brawls, he won—too handily for Pea-Jacket to challenge him. So at 26 he formally entered political life as one of the three council members from Ward 17.

With his defeat of the aging Pea-Jacket, Curley consolidated himself as the new ward boss, organizing Ward 17 on the Tammany model of tribute and social services and even calling his organization the Tammany Club. There was, however, this difference: Curley's organization was personal rather than self-perpetuating. In politics he would always be a lone wolf.

From that time on Curley never lacked for money. Merchants, tradesmen, and those who did business in Ward 17 now paid to him on a more regulated basis what they had paid to Pea-

WIDE WORLD PHOTO

One of Curley's chief Boston opponents was the late William Cardinal O'Connell, who felt Curley's chicanery cheapened the Irish Catholic heritage the two had in common.

Jacket. But from the ordinary people of the ward, deserving and otherwise, whose needs and requests Curley took care of quickly and efficiently, he expected nothing in gratitude but their votes. When Honey Fitz was mayor of Boston everybody in City Hall paid, from department heads down to the porters and scrubwomen. Curley, gaudy as he might be in his later plundering, never took from the little men. Money came into his hands and slipped through his fingers. For him it was never an end in itself.

The core of his support would always come from the slums. There he was given an allegiance the Pea-Jackets could never command. But Curley never had a political philosophy beyond that of taking care of himself and his own. With equal ease he could at various times support Al Smith, Franklin Roosevelt, Mussolini, Father Coughlin, and Senator McCarthy. If he had had the vision, he might have become to Boston and Massachusetts what Al Smith was to New York. His vision, however, was limited to his own drive for power.

With Ward 17 in his pocket, Curley moved on to the Massachusetts legislature, where he spent one term, more as an observer of the political passing show than as a participant. He was still learning. At the Staley College of the Spoken Word he took elocution lessons, modifying his speech still further to its final form. The Curley accent was unique, with grandiloquent overtones, impressive and at once identifiable, yet underneath synthetic. It achieved the desired effect, but it never rang true. And in an election pinch, it could always be dropped for something more primitive.

In 1903 Curley met his first reverse. He was caught impersonating one of his less talented ward workers at a Civil Service examination and sentenced to sixty days in the Charles Street jail. Yet far from being disconcerted by this lapse he capitalized on it. In later years he often planted stooges in his audience to get up and ask: "How about the time you went to jail?" Curley then liked to draw himself up and announce floridly: "I did it for a friend." Ward 17 understood. While in jail, where he spent a not unpleasant two months reading all the books in the library, he was elected to the Board of Aldermen, the upper chamber of Boston's city government.

Curley remained an alderman until 1909, when he became a member of the new City Council. And all the time he was laying his lines carefully toward his own clear though unexpressed goal—to be mayor and boss of Boston. His retentive mind had the city and its departments catalogued for future use. No one would ever be able to fool Curley.

Established in his thirty-second year, he now found

time to marry Mary Herlihy, whom he had met at a St. Philip's minstrel show. With a background much like his own, she was a woman of grace and character, and a permanently steadying influence on him. It was a happy marriage for them both and a fortunate one for him. Honey Fitz's blond Tootles might become the subject of limericks, still repeated today by elderly Boston politicians, but no enemy could ever touch Jim Curley that way. His private life was always beyond reproach, though it ended sadly, for of his nine children only two survived him.

In 1909 Fitzgerald was elected to a four-year term under Boston's reform charter, which gave him almost complete responsibility. In 1880 Mayor Frederick O. Prince had said: "No allegation of municipal corruption has ever been made against any Boston official." By Honey Fitz's time such a remark could be considered a flat, cynical joke. Another class had emerged to take over the city. These Irish-Americans, more and more of them now second-generation, felt no obligation to observe the rules made by the Beacon Hill ascendancy that had exploited them for the last sixty years. All the other roads had been barred to their strength and their cunning and their enterprise except the road of politics, which they had pushed into by their weight of numbers.

Nobody understood this better than Curley. Contemptuous of Honey Fitz, willing to wait for the next round, he let himself be persuaded to run for Congress by the district incumbent, Bill McNary, who counted on insuring his own re-election by having Curley split his opponent's vote. For the first time Curley stumped outside Ward 17. In a day when political rallies were still a prime source of entertainment, Curley put on a campaign that was a combination of vaudeville, Chautauqua, and the prize ring. No one, his opponents realized too late, could equal him as a showman; no one could talk him down. There was the usual torchlight parade with the bands blaring "Tammany" to celebrate his victory.

He spent two undistinguished terms in the House and his week ends back in Roxbury. In Washington he and his wife mixed in a more sophisticated society than they had known before. They took instruction in etiquette, and this became a source of later jokes in Boston. In his autobiography Curley maintained that he liked Washington. But Boston, the hard core of the

CONTINUED ON PAGE 85

Sharing a distinction granted to only three others in the long history of the Commonwealth, James Michael Curley, dead at 83, lay in state in the Hall of Flags in the Massachusetts State House while thousands of his supporters filed by in silent tribute. Thus even in death the parvenu Irishman had the better of his Beacon Hill adversaries.

BOSTON *Globe*

Pentecost in the Backwoods

Shocking, exuberant, exalted, the camp meeting answered the pioneers'

demand for religion and helped shape the character of the West

By BERNARD A. WEISBERGER

The Great Revival in the West, or the Kentucky Revival of 1800, as it was sometimes called, was a landmark in American history. It was not some accidental outburst of religious hysteria that crackled through the clearings. Rather, it was one of many answers to a question on which America's destiny hung during Thomas Jefferson's Presidency. Which way would the West go? It was filling up fast in 1800, and yet it still remained isolated behind the mountain barriers, only thinly linked to the nation by a cranky, awkward, and dangerous transportation "system" of trails and rivers. Could it be held within the bounds of American institutions as they had developed over 175 colonial years? Would its raw energies pull it into some new orbit—say, an independent confederation? Or, if it stayed in the Union, would it send representatives swarming back eastward to crush old patterns under the weight of numbers?

No group asked this question more anxiously than eastern clergymen. For, in 1800, they saw that their particular pattern was being abandoned on the frontier. From Kentucky, Tennessee, the western Carolinas, and Virginia, reports came back of a world that was shaggy, vicious, and churchless. The hard-living men and women of the forest clearings were not raising temples to God. Their morals (to eastern eyes) were parlous. Corn liquor flowed freely; marriages were celebrated long after children had arrived;

gun and rope settled far too many legal disputes. The West was crowded with Sabbath-breakers and profane swearers, thieves, murderers, and blasphemers, with neither courts of law nor public opinion to raise a rebuke. The whole region seemed "hair-hung and breeze-shaken" over Hell's vault. And this was a matter of life-or-death seriousness to the churches. It was clear even then that America's future lay beyond the mountains. And if the West grew up Godless, then the entire nation would one day turn from His ways, to its destruction. It was no wonder that pious folk of the seaboard dug into their pocketbooks to scrape up funds for "home missionary" societies aimed at paying the way of parsons traveling westward. Or that church assemblies warned of crises ahead and called for special days of fasting, humiliation, and prayer for the West.

Yet, for a fact, the easterners were wrong. They misjudged their pioneers. Western people wanted and needed the church just as badly as the church needed their support for survival. Religion had a part to play in the hard-driven lives of the frontier settlers. It was more than a mere foundation for morality. It offered the hope of a bright future, shining beyond the dirt-floored, hog-and-hominy present. It offered an emotional outlet for lives ringed with inhibition. It was a social thing, too, furnishing occasions on which to lay aside axe and gun and skillet and gather with neighbors, to sing, to weep, to pray, or simply to talk

Jacques Gerard Milbert, a Parisian, painted these scenes of rural revivalism while visiting America. Above, Methodists are carrying bundles of food and clothing with them to a meeting in the woods. Tents, a clearing, and a platform for the preachers were all the equipment needed for a camp meeting. Below, the man on the ground appears to have been seized by one of the ecstasies that affected many.

with others. The West had to have religion—but religion of its own special kind. The West was not "lost" in 1800, but on the verge of being saved. Only it was going to be saved the same way it did everything else: on its own individualistic terms.

The East found this hard to understand. The East had trouble taking stock of such a man as the father of the western revival, James McGready. McGready was an angular, black-eyed Scotch-Irishman, born on the Pennsylvania frontier. He came of a hard-working and pious stock that had filled the western stretches of the Colonies in the sixty years before the Revolution. McGready was true to the spirit of his Highland Calvinistic ancestors, who worked, prayed, and fought heartily. He grew to adolescence without becoming a swearer, drinker, or Sabbath-breaker, which made him something of a God-fearing rarity among frontier youth. So his family sent him to a private school conducted by a minister, where he wrestled with Scripture in the morning and did farm chores in the afternoon for his "tuition." In 1788, he was licensed to preach, and came down to western North Carolina's Guilford County, where his family had moved. Thus, McGready was a product of western Presbyterianism.

That was important. In the 1790's, the religious picture in the United States already showed considerable (and characteristic) variety. Episcopalianism was solidly rooted among the landed gentry of the South. The Dutch Reformed Church carried on the heritage established when the flag of Holland flapped over New York. Various shoots of Lutheranism pushed up out of the soil of German settlements. Baptism and Methodism were small but growing faiths. There were little wedges in the pie of church membership labeled "Quaker," "Catholic," and "Jewish." A few bold souls called themselves Deists. A few more were on the way to becoming Unitarians. American worship wore a coat of many colors. But in New England and the mid-Atlantic states, the Presbyterian and Congregational bodies were unquestionably in the forefront. Both were rooted in the preceding century's Puritanism. Both officially believed in "predestination" and "limited election"—God had chosen a few individuals to be saved from general damnation, and the list, made up from the beginning of eternity, was unchangeable. These chosen "saints" were born in sin, but in His own way God would convert them to holiness during their lifetimes. Meanwhile, the laws of God must be interpreted and explained to mankind. In order to do this, the Presbyterians and Congregationalists had raised up colleges to train their ministers, the most famous among them by 1800 being Harvard, Yale, and Princeton. Graduates of these schools thundered of Jehovah's wrath to their congregations in two-hour sermons rich with samples of their learning. During the week they warmed their study chairs ten hours a day, writing black-bound volumes of theology.

Religion of this sort lacked appeal for the Scotch-Irish migrants pushing into the frontier regions. They were Presbyterians in name. But their wild surroundings did something to them. They came to resent authority—whether exercised by excise collectors, land speculators, lawyers, or, finally, ministers. What was more, they wanted a little stronger assurance of salvation than a strict reading of limited election gave them. There was a need, in this fur-capped, bewhiskered Christian world, for more promise in life, and more passion too. Learned pulpit lectures might do for townspeople, but not for pioneers.

Among common folk, both East *and* West, a ferment of resentment against the "aristocratic" notion of election was at work. In the 1740's it had exploded in a revival called the Great Awakening. Baptist, Presbyterian, Congregationalist, Anglican, and Dutch-Reformed Christians were caught up in a common whirlwind of handclapping, shouting, and hosannaing. A good many new leaders, and a number of unpleasant schisms, had risen out of this storm. And in western Pennsylvania, revival-minded Presbyterians had founded a number of little academies to train their preachers. Derisively dubbed "log colleges" by the learned, they took the name proudly. Their graduates were short on Greek and exegesis but long on zeal. When the Great Awakening sputtered out before the Revolution, these colleges remained, helping to keep the sparks alive. Now, with the new nation established, the fire was ready to blaze again. McGready, himself a log-college graduate, was one of the first to blow on it.

McGready got to grips with the powers of darkness in North Carolina without wasting any time. He began to preach against the "formality and deadness" of the local churches. Besides that, he demanded some concrete testimony of good living from his flock, and the particular evidence he asked for was highly exacting. The new preacher insisted that strong drink was a slippery path to Hell. In Guilford County this did not sit well. Frontiersmen saw no harm in lightening a hard life with a dram or two, and they wanted no lectures on the subject from men of the cloth. In point of fact, there was no cloth. Pioneer ministers wore buckskin, and took their turn with the next man at hoeing corn or splitting kindling. McGready got nowhere—at least nowhere in North

Carolina. After a futile battle, he left to seek a more promising future in Kentucky—some said by request of the congregation.

In Kentucky, circumstances were riper for him. Despite eastern concern, a new Christian community was taking shape in that rugged, bear-and-savage-haunted wilderness province, where crude living went along with high dreaming. It was a community ready to be stirred into life, and McGready was the man to seize the stick. In Logan County, in the southwestern part of the state—a region well-known for unregen-

Barton W. Stone, inspired by James McGready, whipped up the 1801 meeting at Cane Ridge.

erate doings—he had three small congregations: at Red River, Gasper River, and Muddy River. He began to preach to these congregations, and he did not deal with such recondite matters as the doctrines contained in Matthew, or their applications. Instead he would "so describe Heaven" that his listeners would "see its glories and long to be there." Then he went on to "array hell and its horrors" so that the wicked would "tremble and quake, imagining a lake of fire and brimstone yawning to overwhelm them." With that brimstone smoking away in the background, McGready struck for bedrock. The whole point of Christianity, for him, was in the conversion of sinners to saints assured of eternal bliss. His question of questions was dagger-sharp: "If I were converted, would I feel it and know it?" A McGready parishioner was not going to be allowed to rest in self-satisfaction merely because he attended worship and avoided the grosser forms of indecency.

Under such spurring, results began to show among the faithful. In 1799, during a service at Gasper River,

many fell to the ground and lay "powerless, groaning, praying and crying for mercy." Women began to scream. Big, tough men sobbed like hysterical children. What could explain this? Simply the fact that belly-deep fear was taking over. For it is well to remember that in those days conversion was the *only* token of salvation. No matter how young one was, no matter how blameless a life he had led, until the moment of transformation one was a sinner, bound for torment. If death stepped in before conversion was completed, babes and grandsires alike sank screaming into a lake of burning pitch—a lake that was not metaphorical, not symbolical, but *real* and eternal. And death on the frontier was always around the corner—in the unexpected arrow, the milk sickness, the carelessly felled tree, the leap of the wounded grizzly. Frontiersmen bottled up their fear of these things usually. It was the price of sanity and survival. But when a religious service provided an acceptable excuse for breaking down the barriers, it was no wonder that men shivered and wept.

After shaking up the dry bones of the Gasper River settlement, McGready moved on in June of 1800 to Red River. He meant to hold a sacramental service, at the end of which church members would take the Lord's Supper together. What he got was something more uncontrolled. In a meetinghouse of undressed logs McGready shared his pulpit with three other Presbyterian ministers. A Methodist preacher was also present. That was not unusual. Frontier preachers were a small band. They knew each other well. A service was a social occasion, and therefore a treat, and several ministers often took part in order to draw it out.

The Presbyterian shepherds did their preaching, and what they said has not come down to us, but they must have dragged a harrow through the congregation's feelings. When John McGee, the Methodist, arose, an awesome hush had fallen on the house. McGee faced a problem. The Methodists were relative newcomers to America, officially on the scene only since 1766. They were frowned on by more established groups, mainly because they gave emotion free rein in their worship. It was not unusual at a Methodist meeting for women to faint, men to shout in strange tongues, and the minister himself to windmill his arms and bawl himself red-faced. For the more formal Presbyterians, such conduct was out of bounds. McGee knew this, and wanted to mind his ecclesiastical manners. But he knew a ripe audience when he saw one, too, and after an apparent debate with himself, he made his move. Rising, he shouted that everyone in the house should submit to "the Lord Omnipotent." Then he began to bounce from backless bench to backless bench, pleading, crying, shouting, shaking,

CONTINUED ON PAGE 77

This view of Norwich, Connecticut, in the 1850's shows the Laurel Hill bridges over the Shetucket River. The one at left carri...

Roofs over Rivers

Time is taking its toll of the romantic covered bridge, where once

you could exchange gossip, argue politics, or court your lady fair

By RICHARD SANDERS ALLEN

...ains of the old Norwich & Worcester line; the one at right was for carriages and pedestrians. Both were used until the 1870's.

For a hundred and fifty years, the covered bridge has been an old American landmark. Today it is becoming increasingly difficult to find even one, but only fifty years ago the traveler encountered countless numbers of them—at cities, villages, and country crossings from Maine to Georgia and west to California.

The village bridge of the past century was the meeting place of town and country. In its dim interior men argued crops and politics while their womenfolk exchanged gossip and recipes and their children exclaimed over the gaudy circus posters that hung in the bridge long after the show had left town.

Out in the countryside a covered bridge was a good place to save a load of hay in a sudden summer shower. Farm boys found favorite fishing spots in its shade. It seemed as though a high-spirited mare could actually read the signs that were posted prominently over the bridge portals: "Five Dollars Fine for Riding or Driving Faster Than a Walk on This Bridge!"; for often as not she would automatically slow to a sedate pace on coming in sight of the cool, timbered passageway. For years the covered bridge was the country cousin to the city amusement park's Tunnel of Love. The longer the bridge, the better. Just ask grandpa why they called them "kissin' bridges."

But how did bridges come to be covered? To provide shelter for the traveler, some say. Others think the housing presented a homey, barnlike appearance to horses, and thus prevented them from shying at the glint of river water. Actually, the explanation is far less romantic: bridges were originally covered, as one old New Hampshire man put it, "ter perteck the underpinnin'," the framed wooden trusswork. With the rot caused by continual wetting and drying thus avoided, covered bridges have continued to give useful service for periods that amaze modern engineering experts.

American bridge-designers did not invent roofs for bridges. From biblical days onward builders have added roofs to their spans. In ancient times the purpose was mostly decoration and the protection of the people who crossed them. In Italy, China, and Mex-

31

Top: In 1927 the swollen Passumpsic at St. Johnsbury, Vermont, swept one bridge downstream into another, destroying both. Above: This Y-shaped span at Zanesville, Ohio, once carried the National Road. Travelers were told: "Go to the middle of the bridge and turn right."

ico today, there are stone bridges with wooden roofs, used as market places. Village carpenters in Switzerland and Germany, however, seem to have been the first to evolve the idea of a roof to protect the timbers of the bridge itself; in heavily forested central Europe, covered bridges were built as far back as the Middle Ages.

Americans did not adopt the covered bridge until after the Revolution. In a fast-expanding country where the main routes of transportation crossed a number of broad rivers, stone bridges were too expensive and took too long to build. Since there were vast uncut forests in the eastern states, the giant virgin timber became the bridgebuilder's material.

The contribution of American designers was the wooden truss, which could carry bridges of a length undreamed of in Europe. The pioneer bridges in America were simple affairs of short trestles set on piles, built to make fat profits from tolls. These were successful in places like Boston, but what sufficed for the placid Charles River was not enough for other coastal cities with swift and navigable streams to be spanned.

The need was for sturdy, longer bridges without intermediate supports.

Some of the best minds of the time set to work on the problem. A bridge to span the Schuylkill River at Philadelphia engaged the attention of political pamphleteer Thomas Paine, for example, and he worked out various models, both in wood and—an unheard-of material for bridges—iron. For lack of money, however, nothing was accomplished. The same project also fascinated Charles Willson Peale, the eminent artist, whose famous museum was devoted to developing many of the arts and sciences. He put a Paine model on display and set about designing one of his own. Peale's plans never got beyond the model stage either, but in 1797 he wrote an "Essay on Building Wooden Bridges," and was awarded the first United States patent for a bridge design. Charles Peale's heart was in invention alone, not in engineering, so he turned over the patent rights to his gifted but ne'er-do-well son Raphael. The younger Peale, who had tried his hand unsuccessfully at many other jobs, attempted to build a full-sized bridge on his father's plan at Beaufort,

32

Left: America's oldest existing covered railroad bridge is at Bennington, New Hampshire. The engine, alas, is no more. Below: "Old Camelback," built by Theodore Burr in 1813–18, spanned the Susquehanna at Harrisburg, Pennsylvania, until 1902. Right: An old car emerges from an even older covered bridge in the Catskills in New York State. Below right: An 1808 Burr bridge at Schenectady, New York, originally unroofed, was suspended on laminated-wood "cables" that sagged as they weathered. Rebuilt and covered in 1830, the bridge continued in active service until 1873.

South Carolina. It collapsed before completion, and Raphael, always ready with an alibi, blamed the failure on "hiring too many Yankee workmen!"

But up in Newburyport, Massachusetts, another "Yankee workman" was more successful. He was Timothy Palmer, a local shipwright's apprentice. Wooden arches, made of huge squared timbers lapped and mortised together, were his answer to the long-span problem, and he became their first successful designer. Palmer must have come across a copy of an old Italian architectural book by Andrea Palladio, who in the 1550's had devised and built arched wooden-truss bridges over tiny Alpine torrents. Timothy Palmer translated the Italian's brainchild into great timber arches made from the giant stands of pine in the New England forests.

Palmer selected his long timbers—sometimes naturally curved—and floated them downstream directly to his bridge sites. He put up three spans over the Merrimack River in Massachusetts, one over the Great Bay of the Piscataqua in New Hampshire, and then went on to conquer the Delaware at Easton, Pennsylvania,

the Potomac at Georgetown, Maryland, and the Schuylkill at Philadelphia.

This last was a showcase for Palmer. The merchants of the city had at last been able to raise enough money to finance the long-wanted bridge, and they spared no expense to make it the pride of Philadelphia. The fresh paint on its lower structure was even sprinkled with stone dust to give the appearance of masonry. Since he wished his timber trusswork to be prominent, Timothy Palmer took a dim view of this at first, but when it was done—at the instigation of Judge Richard Peters—he graciously allowed that perhaps the bridge *might* last "thirty or forty" years as a result of the extra protection from the weather. (Actually, it lasted forty-five.) Finished in 1805, it was dubbed the "Permanent Bridge"; its arched roadway stretched across the Schuylkill in three spans for a total length of 550 feet. It was the first known covered bridge in America.

In 1812, another bridgebuilder got his start at Philadelphia. He was Lewis Wernwag, a German immigrant and designer extraordinary. At Fairmount he planned and erected a monstrous bridge across the Schuylkill

33

Above: Typical of Oregon's austere bridges is the Thornton Creek span in Lincoln County, erected in the early 1920's.

with a single span of 340 feet, far and away a record for that day. As it neared completion, reports began to circulate that it would fall as soon as the scaffolding was removed. Soon the rumors were rife, and on the morning of the day set for the removal of the false-work, thousands jammed the banks of the river to see the expected collapse.

The bridge-company managers were naturally worried, and assembled on the porch of Sheridan's Tavern nearby. When Wernwag arrived, their first words were: "Well, Lewis, do you think our bridge will stand the test today?"

Wernwag smiled and replied: "Yes, gentlemen, it will." Then he led them out on the new-laid planking and showed them the blocks and wedges on which the arches rested. They were all loose; Wernwag had

TEXT CONTINUED ON PAGE 82
ILLUSTRATIONS CONTINUED ON FOLLOWING PAGES

34

The Poetry of Bridgebuilding

In 1949 townspeople of Charlemont, Massachusetts, appealed—in somewhat creaky verse—to the state's Department of Public Works to replace in kind a covered bridge:

> The Bissell Bridge is falling down,
> Right in the middle of our town
> Please view the matter with alarm
> And do vote "Yes" unto our plan.

As related in Richard Sanders Allen's Covered Bridges of the Northeast, *the department replied—also in kind:*

> Struck by the setting's natural beauty
> The Commissioner said 'twas the state's duty
> To save that lovely rustic view
> And save the state some money, too.
> For it seems the wood bridge can compete
> And still be cheaper than concrete . . .

The new bridge is pictured at top left on the facing page.

As described on the opposite page, the Bissell Bridge in Charlemont, Massachusetts, was built in 1951 by the state.

This covered bridge crosses Laurel Hill Creek at the hamlet of Metzler, Upper Turkeyfoot Township, Pennsylvania.

America's only covered wooden aqueduct—restored in 1946—takes Whitewater Canal over a creek at Metamora, Indiana.

Mill Village Bridge near Rutland, built by famed Vermont designer Nicholas Powers, stood nearly a century—until 1947.

One of Oregon's relatively new spans—it was built in 1938—is Goodpasture Bridge over the McKenzie in Lane County.

In 1954 Ware, Massachusetts, rebuilt its half of Gilbertville Bridge; adjoining Hardwick put the job off for a while.

Accidents, Old Age, and

the Rush of Progress

Doom the Covered Bridge

While the roof and sides of a covered bridge help preserve its roadbed and underpinning from rain and snow, they are scant protection against rampaging floods. That of November, 1927, for example, demolished about 200 bridges in Vermont alone (see page 32). Other reasons for the disappearance of the covered bridge are illustrated on these two pages. Above: A rare photograph of 1865 shows what happened when a Rensselaer & Saratoga locomotive, the Jay Gould, backed out of a covered bridge at Troy, New York, into an open draw. Age and neglect combined to destroy the span at top left on the opposite page. It was located in Bedford County, Pennsylvania, and has now been replaced. Next to it is Cameron Bridge across West Canada Creek, near Gravesville, New York. This one was purposely burned in 1937 after the road leading to it had been abandoned, but accidental fires spelled the doom of hundreds of covered bridges. It is the urge for speed in travel, however, symbolized by the photograph at right, which is decimating the ranks of the country's covered bridges most relentlessly. Beneath the graceless girders of what New York unfortunately chooses to call its "Thruway" over Wall Kill at Rifton is little Perrine's Bridge, which has spanned the kill for 109 years. Now, like most of its wooden brothers, it is little more than a nostalgic reminder of America's more leisurely past.

When Benjamin Franklin came home from France

in diplomatic triumph, he left behind a lovely,

highborn lady mourning the miles between them

"We shall eat apples

You combine with the best heart, when you wish, the soundest moral teaching, a lively imagination, and that droll roguishness which shows that the wisest of men allows his wisdom to be perpetually broken against the rocks of femininity." It is not Ben Franklin the essayist or philomath or pamphleteer that Madame d'Hardancourt Brillon de Jouy is here praising, though in these areas his accomplishment had been substantial, but Franklin the letter writer. He in turn always found her letters a delightful contrast to the written requests that endlessly beset him at the American Embassy in Paris. Between 1777 and 1789 they exchanged over 150 letters and several bagatelles and poems, all of them in French except his final letter, in which (one hastens to add) he demonstrated a wit, tact, and sympathy that equaled hers. This correspondence, more than half of it still unpublished, is now among the Franklin Papers at the American Philosophical Society in Philadelphia.

Chauncey Tinker wisely observes that "a letter is, by its very nature, not addressed to an audience, but to an individual; and as certainly as it becomes general in its appeal, it loses that intimacy of tone which is its peculiar charm." The vitality of this correspondence between the sage American who was more than seventy and the beautiful French woman not yet forty lies in just such intimacy; its charm seems at times too fragile, as if gazing too long would dispel it altogether. An eavesdropper is persuaded that these two human beings, for all their difference in age, background, and temperament, were so nearly attuned that there sometimes occurred that almost unconscious transference of mind to mind which Dr. Johnson calls the supreme skill in letter writing.

At the end of 1776, Franklin sailed from Philadelphia, commissioned by the Congress to help nego-

tiate a treaty of alliance with France; successful in this, he continued at Paris, serving as minister plenipotentiary even beyond the war's end. So relentless were the demands of his post that not once in the nine years he was there did he leave the capital and its suburbs; as a consequence, he probably "saw little of France except the best of her"—his biographer James Parton is speaking—"her most enlightened men, her most pleasing women, her most pleasant places." Throughout these years he lived at suburban Passy, "in a fine airy House upon a Hill, which has a large Garden with fine Walks in it," where "I have abundance of acquaintance, dine abroad six days in seven."

Settling down in the midst of an ever-widening circle of friends, he soon felt rejuvenated; so much so that in 1780 he tells an old friend, "Being arrived at seventy [his age when he came to France], and considering that by travelling further in the same road I should probably be led to the grave, I stopped short, turned about, and walked back again; which having done these four years, you may now call me sixty-six." In particular he was disposed, despite his uncertain French, to find stimulating the atmosphere of salons like that held by Madame Helvétius at nearby Auteuil. Rousseau has characterized salon conversation as flowing easily and naturally,

neither dull nor frivolous, full of knowledge without being pedantic, gay but not noisy, polished without affectation, gallant and not merely insipid, playful but not ambiguous. Everything is discussed in order that every one may be able to say something, but no subject is plumbed to its depth for fear of becoming tedious. It is brought up quite by the way and rapidly disposed of, but precision gives an elegance to conversation in that every one gives his opinion in as few words as possible. No one attacks another's point of view with warmth, and the latter does not defend it

of paradise..."

By BRUCE INGHAM GRANGER

with any obstinacy. People indulge in discussion in order to enlighten themselves, but stop before it can degenerate into a dispute.

If one allows for the more clearly self-conscious posture of the French salon, this characterization goes far toward defining the special charm of the letters which passed between Franklin and Madame Brillon.

She was 36 when Franklin met her in 1777. Her marriage to a treasury official 24 years her senior, judging by the tone of her letters, was one of convenience. "I know," she confides, "that the man to whom my fate has bound me is a worthy person; I respect him as I should and as he deserves; perhaps my capacity for affection is too great for his heart to respond to." And then, concerned for the happiness of her daughters: "We marry a young girl whose heart overflows with youth and its burning desires, to a man in whom all such feelings are extinct. We demand of this woman a perfect propriety. My friend, that is my story and that of how many others!"

She admitted to an "excessive sensitiveness" that made her "often the victim of a too tender soul and a too lively imagination." Her physical condition, "which a mere whiff of air upsets," kept her to her bed for long periods, and because of it she frequently went to the country. One year she wintered at Nice, an "eternal springtime" where her health and spirits revived. But she was most at home amidst the social round at Passy: tea, music, chess, visiting and receiving friends. And now there was Franklin. Having lost her own father early in life, she begs him, "Never call me anything but 'my daughter.'" He in his lonely widower's existence 3,000 miles from home and family was very pleased to accept the role.

Whenever, as sometimes happened, he abandoned it to pursue a tactful but aggressive courtship under the not-jealous eye of her husband, she checked him. Once he tells a story to demonstrate the force of his love. "A Beggar asked a rich Bishop for a Louis as Alms—You are mad. One does not give Louis to beggars—A crown then—No, it is too much—Then a farthing—or your blessing—My blessing! Yes, I will give it to you—No, I will not accept it, for if it were worth a farthing you would not give it to me." "That," he urges, "is your charity to a poor unfortunate, who formerly enjoyed affluence and who is unhappily reduced to beg Alms of you." "You adopted me as your daughter," she chides, "I chose you for my father: what do you expect from me? Friendship! well, I love you as a daughter should love her father . . . whatever you may think or say, no one in this world loves you more than I."

Wednesdays and Saturdays, when the weather was mild and health permitted, Franklin visited the Brillon home in the afternoon, where "with her daughters, who sing prettily, and some friends who play, she kindly entertains me and my grandson with little concerts, a cup of tea, and a game of chess." In "The Ephemera," one of the bagatelles addressed to her, he declares that two of the solid pleasures remaining to him, an "old grey-headed" fly, are "the pleasant conversation of a few good lady ephemerae, and now and then a sweet smile and a tune from the ever amiable *Brillante.*"

Their affection was mutual and abiding. She maintains that her loving him tenderly is better than his loving her furiously and too much. Late in their friendship he confesses that since he must one day leave for America with no hope of seeing her again, he has thought of severing with her gradually by seeing her less and less often, but finding that this augments rather than diminishes the desire to be in her company, he would come see her that night. Well she knew, though, that she must share his heart with other women, especially with her "amiable and formidable rival," Madame Helvétius, widow of the famous *philosophe*, who claimed his Saturdays the winter Madame Brillon spent at Nice.

In 1781 Franklin, anxious to strengthen the bond of friendship, anxious too for a real home, proposed a marriage between Madame Brillon's eldest daughter, Cunegonde, and his grandson Temple, the natural son of his natural son William. Both she and her husband realized there were differences in religion and circumstance that could not be overcome, though she adds tactfully, "what it has cost us to refuse it, should assure you forever of our affection." This rejection did not alter the affection between the two families. Two years later Cunegonde married a Monsieur Paris, and when her first child was born, Franklin shares in Madame Brillon's happiness: "I remember that I one day met at your house four generations of your family, when your children were very young, and that I then said that I hoped to live to see the fifth. And here my prophetic wish is realized."

"Your letter, my kind Papa," she graciously replies, "has given me keen pleasure; but if you would give me a greater, remain in France until you see my sixth generation. I only ask you for fifteen or sixteen years: my granddaughter will be marriageable early; she is fine and strong."

For more than half a century Franklin had been corresponding extensively, with family, friends, and the officialdom of two continents, but now when he was writing in a foreign tongue, he suddenly felt unsure of his grammar and idiom. At his request Madame Brillon obligingly corrected his mistakes, but did so sparingly; in her eyes what he called *"beaucoup de très mauvais français"* only enhanced his style. It angered her to see how another, perhaps his friend Abbé de La Roche, had corrected his "Dialogue with the Gout." "Believe me," she advises him, "leave your works as they are, use words that say things, and laugh at grammarians, who, by their purity, weaken all your sentences."

The wonder is that with the constant official demands on his time he was able to address as many as thirty letters to her, and four bagatelles: "The Ephemera," "The Morals of Chess," "The Whistle," and "Dialogue Between Franklin and the Gout." She, having more time at her disposal, sent him more than 120 letters and three original poems. She sensed the danger of revising her own work too much. "I have corrected some faults in the fable," she says of one of her poems; "there are many more yet to be corrected. But I fear that I might resemble the sculptor who, finding the nose on a fancied face a little too large, took away so much that no nose remained." Grammatical roughness, an urbane tone, and frequent wit mark both sides of the correspondence, but his is decidedly the more didactic.

Let us now eavesdrop, first as they exchange thoughts on the gout. Since Franklin and later her husband suffered violent attacks, this was no theoretical subject, like some they chose to discuss. During a severe attack in October, 1780, Franklin received her poem, *"Le Sage et la Goutte,"* which he eventually had printed on his private press. The poem seems clearly to have helped inspire his famous Dialogue; in both pieces, and hers was probably written earlier, the Gout charges that the Sage eats too much, covets the ladies, no longer walks abroad, and spends his time playing chess. Franklin praises her poem but adds:

One of the personages of your fable, Gout, seems to me to reason pretty well, with the exception of the supposition that mistresses have had a share in producing this painful malady. I believe the contrary, and this is my argument. When I was a young man and enjoyed more of the favors of the sex than I do at present, I had no gout. So if the ladies of Passy had had more of that kind of Christian charity that I have so often in vain recommended to you, I should not have had the gout at all. This seems to me good logic.

She is quick to retaliate that there is no logical connection between a man's moral condition and natural events: "THEN you could have had the gout without having deserved it, and you could have well deserved it, as I believe, and not have had it." Several years later she asks him, heretic though he is, to pray for her gout-ridden husband. "I am vexed with Madame Gout for afflicting our friend," he replies. Then, alluding to his Dialogue: "You know that she formerly gave me some good advice. But, unhappily lacking the energy to profit by it, I can do no more, it seems to me, than send it to our friend, to whom it might perhaps be useful." Roguishly he concludes, "If God loves you as much as I love you, my prayers will be useless and superfluous. And heretic as I am, I do not doubt that He loves such Catholics as you."

If she could banter about the gout, it was otherwise when her sensitive nature was hurt. What caused her perhaps the greatest pain was the knowledge that her husband was having an affair with their daughters' governess, Mademoiselle Jupin. In agitation she writes Franklin: *My* life, my friend, is made of fine and thin stuff, that grief tears cruelly; . . . . cure me, or pity me, if you can do one and the other." "To be sensible of our own faults is good," comes his wise reply,

THE OLD PRINT SHOP

Franklin's reception at Versailles in March, 1778, by Louis XVI and Marie Antoinette (seated, right) set the royal seal of approval on the American's already growing popularity in France. Shortly afterward John Adams arrived and noted: "The reputation of Franklin was more universal than that of Leibnitz or Newton, of Frederick II or Voltaire . . ." Here the Comtesse de Polignac crowns Franklin with laurel as the court looks on.

"for it leads us to avoid them in the future; but to be too sensitive to, and afflicted by, the faults of other people is not good." When in a more prudential mood still he suggests that "we might all draw more good from [this world] than we do and suffer less Evil, if we would but take care not to give too much for our Whistles," she replies—and the letter exposes her overgenerous nature—that she has paid dearly for bad whistles, with her heart if not with her purse, that (for example) in loving others she has rarely received the value she gave.

In this crisis and in others, Franklin's wisdom strengthened her in her agonized existence, and his sympathy made life endurable. Nowhere is this wisdom, which she never felt she could achieve, expressed more efficiently than in the following letter.

I think with you, that there are many hardships in life. But it seems to me that there are many more pleasures. That is why I love to live. We must not blame Providence inconsiderately. Reflect how many even of our duties it has ordained to be naturally pleasures; and that it has had the goodness, besides, to give the name of sin to several of them so that we might enjoy them the more.

It is a sanguine answer to one who was melancholy by nature.

What highlights the correspondence, though, is the thrust and parry of verbal courtship. When he asks her to undertake his conversion, she finds him guilty of only one capital sin—covetousness; but, knowing his frailties, she will show mercy. "Provided he loves God, America and myself above all else, I absolve him from all his sins, present, past and future, and promise him a heaven whither I will lead him along a pathway strewn with roses." In rapture at the prospect of being absolved of the future, he pleads guilty to coveting his neighbor's wife but asks whether his keeping religiously the two additional Commandments he has been taught is not sufficient compensation: "The first was: Increase and multiply and replenish the earth. The twelfth is, . . . *that you love one another.*" She dare not decide the question "without consulting the neighbor whose wife you covet, because he is a far better casuist than I am; and then, too, as Bonhomme Richard would say: *In weighty matters, two heads are better than one.*"

During her absence at Nice his thoughts once again

41

THE GLORIOUS

It was a day when all the rules were off, and danger was part of the fun

When laws against the use of fireworks became prevalent, they put an end to an American institution that once was firmly built into every boy's life, making patriotism seem a joyous and understandable thing. Youngsters today do not even know the phrase, yet it was not so many years ago that a "Glorious Fourth" was as much a part of the calendar as a Happy New Year or a Merry Christmas.

The Fourth I remember best took place in 1920. I was eleven; security had returned forever to a world that had recently finished the war to end wars; the country was conscious of its strength and proud of the tradition the Fourth stood for. Everything was ripe for a Glorious Fourth.

Early in June we had begun to make our plans, because fireworks cost money and money therefore had to be earned. There was a good deal of lawn-mowing and errand-running, and the movies had to get along for a while without our eleven-cent admission fees. Then, a few days ahead, temporary shacks of corrugated sheet metal began to go up in empty downtown lots, and paper signs with bold red letters saying FIREWORKS were pasted to their sides.

As we lined up to buy, most of us had lists to follow. We wanted the largest possible amount of noise for our money, so as a rule we invested heavily in the biggest salutes the law would allow. Then we bought Chinese firecrackers, the kind that came in red tissue-wrapped packages with a bright label containing a fierce dragon and exotic Chinese characters. These firecrackers ranged in size from two or three inches down to little inch-long ones not much thicker than a pencil lead, which we usually set off a whole package at a time.

We also bought torpedoes, snakes, pieces for night use, and the items inconsiderately known as "niggerchasers"; the latter, when lighted, sizzled on a zigzag course as if in pursuit of a victim. Torpedoes were caps screwed tightly together with a bunch of pebbles into a piece of tissue paper. When you threw them against a wall or sidewalk they went off—usually.

We bought snakes because, amidst much noise that left nothing to the imagination, they were silent and something of a mystery. They looked like small white pills, yet when you lighted one it would begin to disgorge a pencil-thin snake that sometimes grew to be a yard long. If you touched it, it crumbled to a powdery ash.

Caps were available in rolls for automatics, but at eleven my friends and I, having grown too old for cops and robbers, left this item to our younger brothers.

The Fourth of July was a male celebration. Women were not expected to have any part in it—except perhaps when mothers were called to bind up burned hands. There was, to be sure, a contraption for girls that shot off caps at the end of a cane, but this was scarcely worth considering. On this one day in the year a boy could satisfy the urge to live dangerously and to make all the noise he could. There was a tacit understanding that, within limits, a boy could work

UNSAFE FOURTH

By BRADFORD SMITH

off the pent-up aggressions and energies that were ordinarily suppressed by the joyless adult rules hemming him in. It was permissible, for instance, to toss a firecracker into the Methodist minister's study window, but not to haul off the church pews for a bonfire. Distinctions like that had to be learned.

When we went to bed on the night before the Fourth, the explosions had already begun. We went to sleep listening to them, and they were sweeter music than any we knew, with their promise of the day to come.

We were up at dawn—there was always competition among us to see who could wake up his friends with the first salute—and from then until bedtime we lived in a world of danger, activity, loud noises, brass bands, runaway horses, and continuous excitement.

The weather was expected to be hot and sunny, and I cannot remember that it ever failed. Even at dawn you could feel the hint of what was to come. It used to get so hot that the tar sidewalks on Main Street often softened, taking the imprint of the watchers who stood there to see the parade.

Our first task was to visit a neighbor marked for our special attention—the school principal. We each lit a firecracker and tossed it at his bedroom window, and then scattered to the nearest trees. Although our attack produced no visible result, we assured ourselves that every cracker had landed squarely on his bed and that we had repaid him for all his restrictions upon our liberties. We also paid our compliments to the old maid who insisted on chasing us out of her apple tree and to a man who had kept our baseball when it had shattered his parlor window.

It was this beautifully simple balancing of accounts that made the Fourth not only a playday, but a way of getting back at the adult world, a way of restoring equilibrium between the warring worlds of men and of boys—the men having the advantage all the year except at Halloween. In this sense every explosion we created had curative value, and every adult expression of annoyance, every headache, every startled movement to get out of the way of our artillery satisfied our deep need of rebelling against the authority that kept us in bondage. Our wounds of war in the shape of burned and blistered fingers were badges of courage in this struggle, and we were very proud of them.

At breakfast my father told us tales of six-inch salutes and of gunpowder packed into small cannons with paper wads and stones, but such evidences of the unrestricted right of Americans to blow themselves to kingdom come had been ruled out by my time. We had to do the best we could with three-inchers. As a matter of fact, a higher form of explosive than mere gunpowder was used in them, so perhaps they were not far from those of my father's youth.

There was drama in every explosion. There was always the chance that no matter how carefully you ignited the fuse, the fire would run to the powder faster than you could run away. Part of the fun, indeed,

CONTINUED ON PAGE 92

ILLUSTRATED FOR AMERICAN HERITAGE BY ARTUR MAROKVIA

New York's Bloodiest Week

The draft riots of 1863 turned

a great city into a living hell

By LAWRENCE LADER

"We shall have trouble before we are through," George Templeton Strong, a wealthy New Yorker and staunch friend of Lincoln, warned in his diary one July morning in 1863. Yet the first nationwide military draft, authorized by Congress on March 3 to fill the critically depleted ranks of the Union Army, began in a festive mood.

At 9 A.M. on Saturday, July 11, the provost marshal of the Ninth Congressional District, first in the city to start its drawing, ascended the platform in his office at 46th Street and Third Avenue. A revolving drum with thousands of tightly rolled slips of paper was spun. The marshal's blindfolded assistant drew the first name—William Jones. The crowd laughed, and someone shouted, "Poor Jones!" Each succeeding name was greeted with similar banter, that of a prominent alderman, undoubtedly expected to buy his way out of the draft under the much-disputed $300 exemption payment, eliciting cries of "There's three hundred for sure!"

Such "good feeling" was the rule of the day, reported the New York *Tribune*. There was no premonition of disaster; only slightly strengthened police patrols at the draft offices. Yet by Monday morning, New York would be torn by the bloodiest riot in its history and would stand on the brink of revolution.

The portents had been gathering for months. New York's Copperhead press—the *Day Book, Express, Freeman's Journal,* and *Daily News* among others—had been attacking the draft furiously. Governor Horatio Seymour himself abetted the attack by insisting the

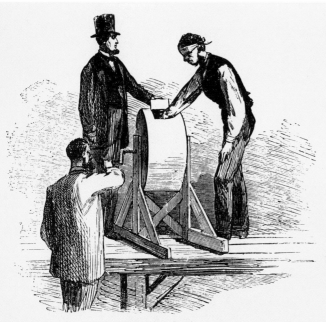

The draft begins.

The spark that touched off the riots was the drawing of the first draftees' names (left) by the Provost Marshal's assistant on Saturday, July 11, 1863. The draft "came like a thunderclap on the people," and by noon Monday rioters had virtually taken over the city. Their primary human victims were New York's Negroes, whose willingness to work for lower wages threatened the jobs of the Irish workers making up the majority of the mobs. The wave of violence finally ebbed on Thursday, but in the bloody meantime it had produced the scenes shown on these pages. Most of them were originally published in Harper's Weekly, Leslie's Illustrated, *and the* Illustrated London News; *several are from the J. Clarence Davies Collection, Museum of the City of New York.*

draft was unconstitutional. A Democrat elected in 1862, he had kept faith with the Union by rushing seventeen regiments of militia to Gettysburg. But his position was equivocal, and in repeatedly demanding that the draft be stopped, he came disturbingly close to the Copperhead line.

There was nothing equivocal, however, about Fernando Wood, former mayor and now a congressman. Elected to Congress in 1863, Wood seized on the draft as the perfect issue to rouse his supporters, mainly Irish immigrants from the Bowery, the docks, and the Five Points tenements. Wood had no trouble inciting great segments of the city's workers. They were already embittered by the two controversial exemption clauses in the Conscription Act. One clause allowed any drafted man to gain release by hiring a suitable substitute. The other allowed any draftee to buy his way out of the Army by paying $300 to the government.

Either escape was far beyond the reach of the average workingman. Even in the inflationary cycle of 1863, he would be lucky to earn $500 a year, making the $300 exemption virtually impossible, the hired substitute a dream. Quite logically, the draft made this "A rich man's war and a poor man's fight." One workingman's letter to the New York *Times* asserted ". . . that $300 has made us nobodies, vagabonds and cast-outs of society. . . . We are the poor rabble and the rich rabble is our enemy by this law. . . ."

The $300 exemption gave Lincoln weeks of agonizing indecision. Finally he drew up a memorandum, summing up the arguments in its favor. Quite clearly his own arguments failed to satisfy him, and in the end he buried the memorandum in his file. The controversial exemption clause was allowed to stand, a fateful monument to political expediency.

The provost marshal's decision to start the drawing in New York on a Saturday was clearly foolhardy. Thousands of workers, with a whole Sunday ahead of them to churn up their bitterness in every corner bar, woke up to find their names listed in the papers. What had seemed only an ominous threat—that very day Governor Seymour had promised to stop the draft by sending his adjutant general to Washington—now became harsh reality.

All that Sunday afternoon New York's East Side was crowded with angry, cursing men. First and Second Avenue bars were jammed. The volunteer fire companies, often unofficial headquarters for the local Democratic machine, were leading centers of unrest. Some companies raised pools to buy exemption for drafted members. Others, like Fire Engine Company No. 33 on 58th Street near Broadway, proudly called "The Roughs," promised more direct action, telling a *Herald* reporter that ". . . if Lincoln attempts to enforce the draft in New York in violation of state authority, there will be black eyes and bloody noses."

Sam Galligan, known as "The Bully Boy" and described by the *Times* as "a well-known wire-puller of the Ward," went from bar to bar, organizing his cronies. The employees of a contracting firm agreed to meet en masse in an empty lot near Central Park early

Police charge rioters at the Tribune *office.*

A mob burns the Negro orphanage at Fifth Avenue and 43rd Street.

Monday morning. The stevedores decided to join them. Southern agents with ready cash, pro-Administration papers claimed later, helped fan the revolt. John Andrews, an aristocratic-looking Virginian, rode a plodding gray mare up and down the East Side streets, corralling friends and giving impromptu addresses at busy corners.

At 10 A.M. on Monday, July 13, Captain Charles Jenkins, the provost marshal, reopened the draft. But there was no hilarity then, only catcalls and hisses as each name was drawn.

Jenkins had drawn about seventy names when a pistol was fired outside his window. Paving stones and brickbats were thrown into the room. The crowd inside grabbed tables and chairs and hurled them at the draft officers. The small police detail barely managed to help Jenkins and his aides escape through the back door. Then the police were overwhelmed. Reported the *Tribune:* "They were knocked down, were beaten with fists, with clubs, with stones . . ." Cans of kerosene were splashed across the floor. A few minutes later the building was in flames, the fire spreading to adjoining buildings on Third Avenue whose upper floors were occupied by women and children.

The clanging fire bell on 51st Street brought Fire Chief John Decker and two loyal engine companies to the scene. They unrolled their hoses, but the howling mob fought them off, threatening to kill them. Decker pleaded with the mob to let him save the rest of the street. But it was more than an hour, and most of the houses were in ruins, before he could use his hoses.

Since ten o'clock emergency messages had been flooding Metropolitan Police Headquarters on Mulberry Street, at the lower end of the city. The police telegraph system connected Superintendent John Kennedy simultaneously with all 32 precincts, and he immediately summoned all reserve platoons to duty. But the mob had cut down the telegraph poles, rendering twelve miles of wire useless and putting Kennedy out of touch with most of the upper half of the city. He decided to drive uptown in his carriage to investigate.

Kennedy had no idea of the extent of the riot until he found himself in the middle of the mob. A handsome, powerfully built man of sixty, he was immediately recognized, attacked, and knocked to the ground. "The mob nearly killed him," the *Tribune* reported. "They beat him, dragged him through the streets by his head, pitched him into a horsepond, rolled him into mud-gutters, dragged him through piles of filth indescribable." Kennedy saved himself only by shouting to a prominent member of the community, John Eagen, on the fringe of the mob. Eagen managed to fight off the attackers while Kennedy raced across a vacant lot to high ground. Here he was cornered and beaten again. By the time a small squad of police arrived, the mob must have thought Kennedy dead. His body was placed on a passing wagon and taken to police headquarters, where he remained under medical care for the rest of the week.

The senior member of the Police Board, Thomas Acton, now took command, conferring immediately with Mayor George Opdyke at City Hall. The defense

A Negro boy is lynched on Eighth Avenue.

Looters put a home on Lexington Avenue to the torch

of the city actually rested in Acton's hands since the state administration in 1857 had vested all power in the Metropolitan Police Board. This turned out well for the city. A police force packed with Fernando Wood appointments might have offered only token resistance to the mob.

With only 800 men on duty that day against a mob that would soon number 50,000, Acton's strategy was to concentrate his force at police headquarters and City Hall to protect the banks, federal installations, major hotels, and stores in the lower half of the city. The futility of limited resistance was already being demonstrated at Third Avenue and 43rd Street, where 44 policemen under Sergeant McCredie of the fifteenth precinct clashed with the mob. Only 5 of the 44 came through unwounded. One officer, after being beaten almost to death with crowbars, was saved by John Eagen's wife, who flung her body on the policeman's to shield him from the mob.

A fifty-man company of the Army's Invalid Corps (wounded veterans now on guard duty, rushed into action because of the shortage of troops) was cut to pieces even more brutally. Marched up Third Avenue, they fired directly into the mob; no one seemed to know whether they used bullets or blank cartridges. Then, fighting with bayonets, the soldiers were surrounded and cut off by hundreds of rioters. A few soldiers tried to flee for their lives, "hunted like dogs," reported the *Times*. One was left dead in the gutter on 41st Street. Another fled to the high rocks near 42nd Street, where he was beaten "almost to a jelly," said the *Tribune*, and tossed over a precipice.

By noon the city was virtually in the hands of the mob. Major General John Wool, commander of the Department of the East, and Brigadier General Harvey Brown, who commanded federal troops in the city, sent desperate messages for help to the Brooklyn Navy Yard, Governor's Island, and federal forts as far away as Massachusetts. The few hundred federal troops in the city had to be stationed at vital points like the arsenal on Elm Street. By midnight the first uniformed reinforcements had arrived: several companies of marines with howitzers and cannon, 300 sailors from the Brooklyn Navy Yard with revolvers and cutlasses, and police reserves from Brooklyn. By early Tuesday morning there were still only a thousand federal troops in the city. Since at least half had to guard federal installations in the lower city, General Brown, who cooperated closely with Acton, could keep only a small force of soldiers at police headquarters to join the police in flying squads against the rioters uptown.

The anger of the mob was now turned in a new direction. Under John Andrews' leadership, they were attacking not only the draft but all symbols of authority and wealth. They swarmed down Lexington Avenue, screaming "Down with the rich!" At 46th Street they plundered three fine homes, then burned them to the ground.

Another group of rioters attacked the provost marshal's office at 29th Street and Broadway, first plundering an expensive jewelry store on the main floor.

mob chases a Negro family through Lexington Avenue back lots.

A priest prevents a murder in 37th Street.

Another mob attacked the armory at Second Avenue and 21st Street, used by the government for the manufacture of rifles. The 35-man Broadway squad fought off the mob for an hour, but when the rioters started to set fire to the building, Acton ordered it abandoned. The police managed to escape by squeezing through a tiny hole in the rear wall and fleeing to the eighteenth precinct police station, where they stripped off their uniforms. The station was later burned to the ground.

The Negro population, numbering less than 15,000, suffered most of all. No Negro dared appear on the street. "Small mobs are chasing isolated Negroes as hounds would chase a fox," Major Edward S. Sanford of the U.S. Military Telegraph Service wired Secretary of War Stanton. Many hotels, fearful of being attacked, displayed large signs: "No Niggers in back!" Abraham Franklin, who supported himself and his mother as a coachman, managed to get to his mother's house on Seventh Avenue to make sure she was safe. They talked a few minutes, then decided to pray together. A group of rioters burst open the door, beat Franklin, and hanged him before his mother's eyes.

Peter Heuston, a 63-year-old Mohawk Indian and army veteran of the Mexican War, was mistaken for a Negro and beaten to death near his home on Roosevelt Street, leaving an orphaned daughter of eight.

The mob's savagery to the Negro sprang from complex motivations—economic, social, and religious. Most of its members were Irish. Comprising over half the city's foreign-born population of 400,000, out of a total of about 814,000, the Irish were the main source of cheap labor, virtually its peon class. Desperately poor and lacking real roots in the community, they had the most to lose from the draft. Further, they were bitterly afraid that even cheaper Negro labor would flood the North if slavery ceased to exist.

All the frustrations and prejudices the Irish had suffered were brought to a boiling point by the draft. At pitiful wages they had slaved on the railroads and canals, had been herded into the most menial jobs as carters and stevedores. Many newspaper ads repeated the popular prejudice: "No Irish need apply." An Irish domestic worker was lucky to earn seven dollars a month. Their crumbling frame tenements in areas like the Five Points were the worst slums in the city. Already pressed to the wall, the Irish could logically view the draft as the final instrument of oppression by the rich. One worker wrote the *Times:* "We love our wives and children more than the rich because we got not much besides them; and we will not go to leave them at home for to starve . . ."

In an objective assessment of the Irish role in the riots, *Harper's Weekly* later pleaded that it "be remembered . . . that in many wards of the city the Irish were during the late riot staunch friends of law and order . . ." Many loyal fire companies were made up of Irishmen. Irish priests opposed the rioters at every step, one risking his life to succor Colonel Henry O'Brien as he was being beaten to death, another persuading a mob not to burn Columbia College at 49th

The death of Colonel Henry O'Brien on Second Avenue.

Secessionist John Andrews harangues the rioters on 46th Street.

Street and Madison Avenue. Most important of all, a large segment of the Metropolitan Police were Irishmen who fought the mob with a bravery and devotion probably unequaled in police history.

In the war itself, four New York Irish regiments made impressive records. A former Irish editor, Brigadier General Francis Thomas Meagher, commanded the Irish Brigade. The Irish distinguished themselves at Antietam and Fredericksburg, losing 471 wounded and dead in the latter battle. Of 144,000 Irishmen in the Union Army, over 51,000 were from New York.

But on that Monday afternoon, unfortunately, their pent-up hatred of the Negro exploded in its most savage form. Its object was the Orphan Asylum for Colored Children, a four-story building on Fifth Avenue and 43rd Street, where 233 children were housed.

"Clamoring around the house like demons," as the *Tribune* described it, the mob burst the door with axes. The children knelt with Superintendent William E. Davis to pray. Then a long line of frightened boys and girls, two of them infants carried in teachers' arms, followed Davis out the rear door.

The mob surged through the building, stripping it bare. Hundreds of beds were carried from the dormitory wing. Women and boys grabbed them and carted them down the avenue—a strange procession that one reporter estimated ran for ten blocks. Carpets, desks, chairs, pictures, books, even the orphans' clothes, were tossed out the windows to the waiting plunderers. Then the handsome building was set on fire.

Fire Chief Decker and two engine companies re- sponded to the call, Decker racing alone into the building, struggling to extinguish the brands tossed by the mob. But rioters followed him, setting new fires. Decker went back, accompanied by six of his men, and put them out again.

This time two dozen rioters grabbed him and would have beaten him to death had not ten firemen rushed to his rescue and warned that their chief would be taken only over their dead bodies. Frustrated, the mob turned suddenly on the Negro children, who huddled in a circle on the corner watching their home go up in flames.

Twenty children were cut off from the main group. "There is little doubt that many and perhaps all of these helpless children would have been murdered in cold blood," reported the *Times*. But a young Irishman on the edge of the crowd, Paddy McCaffrey, aided by two drivers from the 42nd Street cross-town bus line and members of Engine Company No. 18, surrounded the children and fought off the mob. While rioters pelted them with stones, they managed to get the children to the thirty-fifth precinct station house. An hour later the orphan asylum was a mess of charred rubble.

Paddy McCaffrey's heroism was one more contradiction of the assumption that all Irishmen supported the rioters.

At the height of the riot that Monday evening, Commissioner Acton got word that the mob was marching on City Hall and police headquarters. Acton decided it was time for the first counteroffensive. He assigned 200 men to Inspector Dan Carpenter, "the Metropoli-

CONTINUED ON PAGE 95

Soldiers and rioters battle at Second Avenue and 22nd Street.

CULVER SERVICE

Federal cavalrymen patrol a city quiet at last.

49

ALL JOIN IN THE CHORUS

For almost two decades at the turn of the century

illustrated songs charmed nickelodeon audiences

By JOHN W. RIPLEY

It is nearly a half-century now since there occurred one of the swifter but less regrettable casualties of American culture—the passing of a form of professional entertainment known as the illustrated song. A strange phenomenon native to music halls, dime museums, vaudeville, and the early, *early* silent movies, the song play, as it was billed in places with pretensions, enjoyed a brief but unforgettable craze during the first dozen years of this century. Today only a few collections of the colored lantern slides that illustrated the songs survive. Yet in 1910, at the peak of the craze, practically every one of the nation's 10,000 movie houses, from the lowly nickelodeons to the plush ten-cent cinema palaces, featured "latest illustrated songs," and employed at least one "illustrator," the distinctive billing accorded to singers who worked with slides.

To members of the music-publishing industry whose patronage accounted for nearly 100 per cent of song-slide production, these "graphics" represented a successful novelty plug for their new songs. To operators of nickelodeons, the illustrated song was a cheap filler, but one ideally suited for that often interminably long "one moment please while the operator changes reels." To the millions of romantically inclined housewives and lovelorn youth addicted to the nickelodeon habit, however, the illustrated song was their trip to Dreamland.

From twelve to sixteen hand-colored, glass photo slides were usually required to illustrate a song, one for each line of lyric. Two additional slides completed a set: one a reproduction of the sheet-music cover; the other containing nothing but the printed words of the chorus over which appeared in bold-faced type, "All Join In The Chorus." In this slide, the least glamorous of the lot, reposed the music publisher's hidden persuader.

The illustrator, having completed his customary solo with picture slides, usually two verses and two choruses, would then signal for the printed chorus-slide to be flashed on the screen, and face up to what was often a thankless and discouraging part of his job—that of leading the community song fest. If by using every trick in his bag he managed to coax an audible minority to join him in as many as three choruses, it was pretty certain that after the show a good number of the audience would be humming, singing, or whistling the tune all the way to their nearest friendly music dealer. Or so the publishers hoped.

Although march songs and comic novelties were successfully illustrated, the ballad, because it unfolded a story, was generally considered best suited for song slides. Whatever its sentiment—sweet or sad—imaginative slide-makers crammed into their 3½ x 4 inch colored transparencies every conceivable angle of syrupy romance or tender pathos. In short, the illustrated song was the purest essence of corn, but corn with an irresistible sales appeal. Properly illustrated, a new ballad stood a fair chance of becoming a success within a few short weeks after the distribution of slides—a fraction of the time required, in those days before radio, to exploit a number in other ways.

When old-timers in the music business talk about the good old days of the illustrated song, you can be certain that they are referring to the music-hall or pre-nickelodeon period. They are not

On the opposite page is a scene in an actual nickelodeon of 1908 located on Third Avenue, New York City. The picture comes from a set of song slides made to illustrate a then-popular ballad, My Moving Picture Babe, *and shows the way things were before VistaVision and Todd-AO. At top above is a cheery "Welcome" slide to make people feel right at home, and below it a teaser to put them in the proper mood to support the illustrated song to come.*

Song slides were interspersed, like modern television, with commercials, previews, and thoughtful messages on such topics as the weather and no spitting on the floor, please.

talking about the "bouncing ball" era of movie-house group-singing that came in the 1920's and has no connection with song slides. In the beginning song slides, for which publishers paid four to five dollars a set, were practically forced on famous singers on a loan basis. By 1908, however, distribution of slides had been turned over to film and slide exchanges, at rental rates ranging from fifty cents to a dollar. Small nickelodeon operators whose clientele wasn't too discriminating could, for a small additional fee, obtain cylinder or disc phonograph records to accompany slides. This earliest form of low-fidelity canned music blared out from giant metal horns, often mounted in pairs, with sufficient volume to be heard in the last row of a 199-seat house. (In certain localities 200 seats or more automatically put the operator in a high license bracket.) The nation's three leading slide-makers, Scott & Van Altena and DeWitt C. Wheeler, both of New York City, and Chicago Transparency Company, Chicago, required a minimum order of fifty sets to start production on illustrations for a new song.

Posing for song slides was considered nice work when one could get it. Production of a set of sixteen 4 x 5 dry-plate negatives was usually accomplished in one day. Most love songs called for a cast of but two models, a "lover" and a "girl," as they were known in the trade. For a day's work each received from three to five dollars, and anonymity; the employers wanted no stars, and no high talent fees.

At least one leading lady of song slides discovered that the work offered a reward more precious than the munificent fees. In her memoirs, the late Norma Talmadge, after she had become one of the great stars of silent films, describes the exquisite joy of seeing herself in a song play, life-sized and in full color, at a neighborhood nickelodeon—her very first screen appearance! The Brooklyn high-school girl, only fourteen at the time (1910), had appeared at Scott & Van Altena's studio in answer to a want ad, "Models wanted for song slides; no experience necessary." Impressed by her mature beauty, Edward Van Altena—today a spry 85 and still actively engaged in making slides for educational and technical purposes—engaged Miss Talmadge as the "girl" in a song-slide production with the arresting title, *Stop, Stop, Stop; Come Over and Love Me Some More.* The song had just been written by a young song plugger-composer employed by the music publisher Ted Snyder. His name was Irving Berlin.

How many other stars of silent films made their screen debuts anonymously via song slides is a matter of speculation. Van Altena, the photographer, and his former partner and master colorist, John D. Scott, recall using at least seven models who later achieved fame in films. Among them were Helene Chadwick, Lillian Walker, Anita Stewart, Priscilla Dean, Mabel Normand, Alice Joyce, and Justine Johnstone.

At that time few observers realized that one particular segment of movie-goers—the recently arrived immigrants from Europe—regarded the nickelodeon as their social club as well as an academy of adult education. Through the "flickers" and song slides these newcomers were introduced not only to American etiquette, styles, and popular music but, more important, to a pleasing and amazingly easy-to-learn course in the English language.

For just five cents those with sufficient fortitude could sit through

At right is a typical line-up of the week's attractions at a ten-cent theater in Topeka, Kansas. The song (item five on the list) that Miss Wayne Clutts was presenting can be viewed in its entirety simply by turning the page.

six or even a dozen consecutive renditions of a song (a complete film show went on every half-hour), and each performance was a visual-education lesson. Eventually, the repeated associations of words and pictures would register on the dullest minds. If it failed to make sense, the language of Tin Pan Alley at least became understandable.

On the old-time vaudeville circuits, popular singers brought the illustrated song to respectable citizens all over the country. Most of these traveling illustrators carried their own projectionists, and for good reason. Even the most proficient of house projectionists, when handling a strange set of slides, might transform a sob into a belly laugh by inadvertently causing a deathbed to appear upside down on the screen.

The foremost illustrator act in vaudeville was the team of Maxwell & Simpson, which gained initial fame with a pathetic "kid" ballad, *Only Me*. In 1904 they added to their repertoire a newly published song about fire-fighters, *The Man with the Ladder and the Hose*, which was soon to become their trademark. Joe Maxwell's fine voice has been preserved on several Edison cylinder records. Simpson, the "lanternist," left the act about 1906 to become a song-slide producer. One of Edison's most popular recording stars, Ada Jones, was regarded as the best illustrator ever to appear at Huber's Museum on Fourteenth Street, New York City, a spot where many name slide-singers regularly appeared. In Chicago, song slides were first introduced "with great success" by Joe E. Howard and Ida Emerson, then his wife, following a tryout of the illustrated-song novelty in Milwaukee. The list of singers who used slides is long, including such stars as George Jessel, Eddie Cantor, and the late Al Jolson.

It was in 1911, while vaudeville was still going strong, that the illustrated song started slipping. A creeping paralysis set in when the parlor piano gave way to a couple of mechanical marvels, the player piano and the improved phonograph. As pianos fell into disuse, sheet-music sales fell off sharply. Then came longer and better motion pictures; and most theaters acquired a second projector to eliminate the delay between reels. The illustrated song was no longer required as a filler. Finally one single solitary song—an illustrated song, too—helped bring on the end. When, in 1911, Irving Berlin's *Alexander's Ragtime Band* began its triumphal march onto the American music scene via the front door, the sentimental illustrated song crept out the back way.

Berlin's new song altered popular music. It wasn't really ragtime, but it was danceable and that, apparently, was just what the public had been waiting for. Tin Pan Alley took up the new rhythm and slide-makers, accustomed to the serenity of the ballad, tried in vain to catch the new spirit. By the end of 1914 song slides were on their way out, to join the spinning wheel and the stereoscope in the national attic.

John W. Ripley, a former staff correspondent and picture editor of Business Week, *now lives in Topeka, Kansas. The illustrations used with this article are from his large collection of song slides produced between 1895 and 1913.*

PICTURE PORTFOLIO CONTINUED ON FOLLOWING PAGES

"Only a Message From Home Sweet Home"

Few ballads provided the slide maker with meatier fare than this sentimental hit of 1905. Carroll Fleming wrote the clichés and Edmond Florant set them to music. The entire set of sixteen slides appears here, with the chorus below. The philosophical may observe that Only a Message *celebrates an abiding item in the credo of the Republic—namely, that city life is evil but that salvation can always be achieved by going back to the farm.*

'Twas in a gay resort one night
There met a reckless crew,

It's only a message from
        Home Sweet Home,
From loved ones down on the farm;

Fond wife and mother,
        sister and brother,
Praying to guard me from harm.

And baby is lisping a prayer tonight
To bless me where-'ere I roam;

Said one,
        "If we had homes like that
We'd all be better men;

And now before you go just read
That letter once again."

It's only a message from
        Home Sweet Home,
From loved ones down on the farm;

CHORUS. *(Slowly, with expression.)*

It's on-ly a mes-sage from Home Sweet Home, From loved ones down on the farm.

Fond wife and moth-er, Sis-ter and bro-ther, Pray-ing to guard me from harm. And

When one said to another, "Jack,
This letter came for you."

"I'll bet it's from a woman, boys,"
Said one among the crowd.

With laugh and jest they
gathered 'round
And Jack replied aloud:

"We'll welcome you Jack,
    If you'll only come back,"
Was the message from
    Home Sweet Home.

"I'm going boys, goodnight,"
    said Jack,
"I know you'll understand."

Then one by one his
    comrades came
And shook him by the hand.

Fond wife and mother,
    sister and brother,
Praying to guard me from harm.

And baby'is lisping a prayer tonight
To bless me where·'ere I roam;

"We'll welcome you Jack,
    If you'll only come back,"
Was the message from
    Home Sweet Home.

ba - by is lisp-ing a prayer to - night To bless me where-e'er I roam, _____ "We'll

wel - come you, Jack, if you'll on - ly come back," Was the mes-sage from Home Sweet Home. _____

Just tell my wife, when you break the news,
I died for a child so fair,
So like our own dear one at home,
With ringlets of golden hair.
Just tell her not to weep for me,
But let her eyes be dry,
And remember I gave my life for one
Too tender and young to die.

The Message of a Dying Engineer* (words by Henry M. Sword, music by Maud Anita Hart) describes the last words of the railroad man who has just rescued this forlorn child at the cost of his life. Children remained successful subjects as long as they were unhappy, unwanted, crippled, or in very poor health.

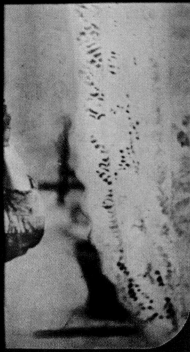

The Engineer is dead and gone

If you're very fond of ringing,
Set the wedding bells a swinging,
Just call around, Just call around,
Ring my door bell when you are alone,
And if you understand
Bring a gold wedding band,
For a ring on the finger
Is worth two on the phone.

A Ring on the Finger is Worth Two on the Phone** (words by Jack Mahoney, music by George W. Meyer) capitalized on a vogue popular since 1901 when Charles K. Harris first penned a little number called Hello, Central, Give Me Heaven. Whether in novelty or sob songs, telephones were sure-fire.

Wait 'till the sun shines, Nellie,
  When the clouds go drifting by,
We will be happy, Nellie,
  Don't you sigh;
Down lover's lane we'll wander,
  Sweethearts, you and I,
Wait 'till the sun shines, Nellie,
  Bye and bye.

Wait Till the Sun Shines Nellie* (*words by Andrew B. Sterling, music by Harry Von Tilzer*) written in 1905, is one of a handful of songs of that time which still enjoy the public's favor. Other familiar relics of the song slide era which still linger on are Down by the Old Mill Stream, Take Me Out to the Ball Game, *and* I Wonder Who's Kissing Her Now.

but sunny Nellie lingers on

Come, my Arab lady,
Where the palms are shady. Hasten to my side
While the stars are beaming, on the sands a gleaming
Swiftly we will ride. You, and I, dear, only
Will not find it lonely. In my tent we'll dwell
Happy we shall be In the desert life so free,
My own Sahara Belle.

My Sahara Belle *testifies to the popularity of Bedouins with bedroom eyes and to the theory, entertained by the song slide pros, that travel is not only broadening but popular with the audiences.*

Half Over

Peril in the Peerless

No song writer worth his salt lets the sun go down on a new invention without weaving it, however painfully, into a new number. Take Me Out For a Joyride* (*words by Ren Shields, music by Kerry Mills*) *and* Try Loving In An Aeroplane (*words by A. Dubin, music by Joseph A. Burke*) *have not outlasted the ancient automobiles and fragile aircraft they celebrated. And the song slide itself, too simple and naïve for a fast-moving age, was doomed. The last illustrated songs were turned out about 1914.*

Take me out for a joy ride, a girl
     ride, a boy ride,
I'm as reckless as I can be. I don't
     care what becomes of me.
Let's go out in the park-way, the
     dark-way, the lark-way,
All afternoon we will spin and spoon
     on an old joy ride.

Try Loving in an Aeroplane.

Won't you sail in the moonbeam's trail,
'Round the moon we can spoon and spoon,
'Way above the clouds where there is no rain,
If you love to love, try loving in an Aeroplane.

Boldness in a Biplane

This Concludes the Performance

Edward Moran's canvas shows Captain Reid's ship, the Armstrong, *under attack by British boats. Fayal's fort is at the left.*

EXPLOIT AT FAYAL

A lonely, gallant battle fought by the designer of our flag

set the stage for Andrew Jackson's victory at New Orleans

By WALLACE C. BAKER

When Andrew Jackson and his triumphant army rode through the streets of New Orleans after crushing Sir Edward Pakenham's veteran troops on January 8, 1815, neither Old Hickory nor his men realized how narrow their margin of victory had been.

Jackson had arrived in New Orleans on December 2 to rally the city's defenses. A few days later, the British under Pakenham and Admiral Sir Alexander Cochrane landed on the Mississippi delta and advanced on the city. What Jackson didn't know was that the British were nearly two weeks behind their invasion schedule.

The doughty Cochrane, fresh from victories in the Chesapeake and the burning of Washington, D.C., had been delayed in assembling his command at Jamaica, British West Indies. The cause for that delay was a train of events set in motion more than two months earlier by one of the most brilliant episodes in American naval history, a sea fight that took place 3,000 miles from the humid Louisiana battlefield.

Few accounts of the New Orleans victory dwell on this crucial ten-day disruption in British invasion plans. Indeed it is a rare student of military history who recalls the inadvertent role of an American privateer in Jackson's triumph.

The drama was played out in the port of Fayal, in the Azores, on the night of September 26, 1814. An American armed brig, the seven-gun, 246-ton *General Armstrong* out of New York, had put in earlier that day at the neutral Portuguese harbor to refill its water casks before harassing English merchantmen along the west coast of Africa.

Aboard the brig was a crew of ninety under the command of Samuel Chester Reid, a young United States Navy officer who had wearied of service on blockaded frigates. Now on its fifth cruise, the *Armstrong* was one of the fastest ships afloat. Among New York's hundred-odd privateers, her record of 24 prizes was second only to the *Scourge*, with 27. On this, her last cruise, she had departed Sandy Hook on September 9 and arrived at Fayal Roads seventeen days later with only one incident—a minor brush with blockading enemy men-of-war.

Her commander, just past thirty, had already been at sea for twenty years, beginning as an eleven-year-old powder boy on an American frigate. His first move after arrival at Fayal was to make a courtesy call on United States consul John B. Dabney, who assured him of the port's neutrality. But ominous news awaited his return to the *Armstrong*.

Three British men-of-war had appeared in his absence and sealed off the port entrance. The first, the 18-gun sloop *Carnation,* sailed into Fayal and dropped anchor a pistol shot away from the American brig. The other two, which Reid recognized as the 74-gun ship-of-the-line razee *Plantagenet* and the 38-gun frigate *Rota,* anchored about a mile away. Thus the British were on the favorable end of exceedingly long odds: to Reid's 7 guns and 90 men they had 130 guns and some 2,000 men.

Word came from Dabney that the squadron was commanded by Captain Robert Lloyd and was en route to the British West Indies—to join up, though Dabney didn't know it, with Cochrane for the assault on New Orleans. Lloyd was a hard-bitten sea dog who only three weeks earlier, in a Fayal café, had boasted that he had boats designed expressly for cutting out American privateers, which he would destroy wherever he found them.

Upon the consul's advice, Reid and his crew warped their ship in under the guns of Fayal's fort and began preparing for the worst. The *Armstrong*'s light draft allowed them to pull within a stone's throw of the shore in waters so shallow that the heavier British ships couldn't come alongside for boarding.

Nevertheless, heavy nets to repel boarders were rigged about the decks. The planking was sanded for sure footing. From the armory below, small arms were brought up and laid out. Buckets of grapeshot were placed by the long nines and the swivel-mounted Long Tom.

As the crew readied the *Armstrong*, they could observe many signal flags being run up on British yardarms and several small boats scurrying about among the three enemy ships.

Shortly after sunset, four armed long boats carrying about 100 men appeared from beyond the *Carnation* and swept toward the American ship. Reid immediately called his men to quarters. Battle lanterns were rigged and gun lamps glowed along the hushed decks.

As the British boats drew within calling distance, Reid challenged them. There was no answer. He could see the British seamen bend strongly on their oars for more speed. Again he warned them to keep their distance.

Still there was no reply. At a wave of Reid's hand, his gunners took careful aim and opened fire with the nine-pounders. Clusters of grape flailed through the boats at close quarters.

The enemy replied immediately. A fusillade of musketry and balls from the light cannon aboard the British long boats beat against the *Armstrong*'s sides. One American seaman crumpled, shot through the heart. Reid's first officer sagged under a musket wound.

Another torrent of grape from the privateer's cannons and the enemy boats were drifting aimlessly under the bow of the *Armstrong*, the slim barrels of a score or more rifles poised above them.

The attackers sued for quarter and the American captain granted it, ordering the British to return to the *Carnation*. He estimated that there were at least twenty dead and wounded among the four boats. What had started out to be a bold cutting-out had turned into a quick repulse for Lloyd, who apparently had hoped to catch the Americans off guard and overawed by the vastly superior force of his squadron.

The British commander ignored the protests of the Portuguese governor of the Azores, Elias Jose Ribeiro, at this breach of neutrality, blandly informing the Governor that his men had been on a peaceful reconnoiter. He went on to state curtly that "one of the boats of his Britannic Majesty's ship under my command was, without the slightest provocation, fired upon. . . . I am determined to take possession of that vessel and hope that you will order your forts to protect the force employed for that purpose."

To Reid's commission as a privateer were attached these orders, signed by Madison's secretary of state, James Monroe.

When informed by Dabney of the exchange of notes, Reid asked the consul's aid in freeing and adding to the *Armstrong*'s crew 32 American seamen interned in Fayal by the Portuguese. The distraught Ribeiro turned down this request and sent fresh appeals to Lloyd.

The moon rose in a clear sky, and residents of Fayal drawn by the earlier firing came down to the shore to watch as the British launched a second attack.

At 9 P.M., the *Carnation* got under way and was observed towing a long line of boats crammed to the gunwales with men. The boats, Reid later reported, "took their stations in three divisions under the covert of a small reef of rocks within about musketshot of us."

Tension mounted on the *Armstrong* as the privateersmen watched the methodical preparations of the large assault force. It was midnight before the British emerged from the protection of the reef. Oars flashed in the bright moonlight as they swept toward the brig. Reid counted at least twelve boats and reckoned the force at about 400 men.

As the strong enemy armada spread out across the harbor, the American sailors waited tensely on the *Armstrong*'s decks. They were a typical cross section of the New York dockside of that day, welded together by the common goal of prize money from a successful cruise. And yet, though they were no heroes to each other, they were to conduct themselves like heroes in the action that lay ahead.

Soon the watchers on the brig could hear the thin cries of the British helmsmen urging on the crews as they came nearer. All eyes aboard the *Armstrong* were on the tall captain pacing the quarter-deck. At last Reid judged that the range was close enough.

"Fire!" he roared. The nine-pounders slammed back against the gun tackles. A storm of grape tore through the packed boats. The screams of the wounded rang out, soon drowned in the crash of the enemy's answering volleys of musket fire and cannon.

From aloft in the brig's rigging, sharp-shooting riflemen took full advantage of the clear night and poured down a murderous fire on the exposed attackers. At close quarters, they picked off enemy officers and helmsmen.

Still the British, with dogged courage, came on. Soon boats were bumping along the sides of the *Armstrong* and under the cannon. Rushing to the sides, the gunners flung cannon balls into the boats, seeking to stave in the bottoms.

A swarm of British seamen poured over the bow and hacked at the boarding nets. In a few moments, the defenders there found themselves engulfed by English cutlasses. Reid, heading the after division, led his yelling men forward as a handful of attackers managed to gain the forecastle.

For several anxious moments, the fighting raged across the narrow decks. Then the British gave way, the survivors plunging over the side to escape the flailing blades of Reid's men.

The slaughter in the boats was appalling. Between the brig and the shore, the harbor waters were dotted with the wreckage of boats and the heads of swimming men. An eyewitness on the shore observed that "some of the boats were left without a single man to row them, others with three or four . . . Several boats floated ashore full of dead bodies. For three days after the battle, we were employed in burying the dead that had washed ashore in the surf."

For his reckless attack, Lloyd paid dearly with the lives of his best officers and bravest seamen. Reid estimated that in the forty minutes from the first American broadside until the last Britisher dove over the side of the *Armstrong*, nearly two-thirds of the assault party were casualties, 120 dead and over 130 wounded. The British captain himself took part in the unhappy affair and suffered a severe leg wound.

Reid's summation of his own situation—in his report of October 4, 1814, to the owners of the *Armstrong*—was a small gem of understatement: "Our deck was now found in much confusion, our Long Tom dismounted, and several of the carriages broken; many of our crew having left the vessel and others disabled." His losses, however, were relatively minor: two killed, seven wounded—all of whom later recovered.

When the Portuguese governor again pleaded for a cessation of hostilities, the raging Lloyd had little patience with formalities. He bluntly stated that he was now determined to have that privateer at the risk of knocking down the entire town.

Throughout the early morning hours, the Americans worked feverishly, remounting their guns and cutting out new positions for them. Useless gear was thrown overboard. At daybreak, the *Carnation* got under way again. Cruising as close to the shallow waters as her commander, Captain George Bentham, dared, the sloop let loose with several broadsides. The privateer replied with its lighter armament.

Many of the *Carnation's* balls passed over the low-lying American brig, but the more accurate fire of the *Armstrong's* gunners paid off. Her hull holed, the *Carnation* hauled off to repair the damage and to replace cut-up rigging and a toppled foretopmast. But her broadsides had had their effect. With most of his topside in complete ruin and several guns out of commission, Reid saw that further resistance was useless. So he had a gun upended and drove a ball through the bottom of the brig. As the *Armstrong* settled in the shallow water, Reid and the surviving crew members swam ashore. British boarding parties took possession of the scuttled brig, and after ascertaining that the task of raising her would take too long, set her afire.

Reid and his crew took refuge in an old convent outside of Fayal. But Lloyd was not content to leave them alone. Chagrined by the fierce resistance and his own heavy losses, he claimed that two of the crew were deserters from the British Navy. British marines, with the reluctant assistance of the Portuguese, rounded up all the privateersmen and marched them down to the town square for interrogation by Lloyd's officers. Even this proved fruitless for the Englishman: he was unable to prove that any of Reid's men were British deserters, and he had to release them all.

The British lingered at Fayal caring for the wounded and retraining men to replace those lost. Three days after the fight, the sloops of war *Thais* and *Calypso* sailed in and were dispatched to carry the more seriously injured back to England. Their captains were cautioned not to release any details of the battle—an indication of Lloyd's worry over his costly victory.

While Lloyd's fleet was thus detained, Cochrane chafed in Jamaica. Lloyd's scheduled arrival date came

Andrew Jackson, the hero of New Orleans, publicly acknowledged that the battle at Fayal was crucial to his victory.

HOW VITAL
WAS REID'S VICTORY?

Historians disagree about how crucial the battle of Fayal was to Jackson's victory at New Orleans. Those of the nineteenth century, among them Benson Lossing, generally agreed with Jackson's sentiments, quoted at the beginning of Mr. Baker's article. Among more recent writers who have taken the same point of view is the late Fletcher Pratt, who in The Compact History of the United States Navy *wrote:*

The victory [at New Orleans] belonged to Andrew Jackson . . . but here also the Navy and the privateers had a part . . . and one single privateer [the *General Armstrong*] delayed the whole expedition by three weeks, which were invaluable to Jackson. That key event took place . . . in the Azores, where the British battleship *Plantagenet,* 74, the frigate *Rota,* 38, and sloop *Carnation,* 18, put in for water, while carrying all the artillery and some of the men for the Louisiana expedition. . . . The attack on that one little privateer cost England more [casualties] than any frigate battle of the war; one hundred seventy-three according to Lloyd's own admission, who did not overstate matters and who forbade his officers to write home about it.

Among those who argue that Reid's battle made little difference is C. S. Forester, author of The Age of Fighting Sail *and many other factual and fictional works dealing with the British and American sailing navies. Mr. Forester says:*

I'm very much afraid that Reid's action at Fayal did not have any effect in delaying the attack on New Orleans. It took place on September 26 and 27; the British attacking force for New Orleans did not appear in American waters until December 8; the British ships at Fayal . . . were not essential to Cochrane's force (I can find no basis whatever for Fletcher Pratt's assertion that they carried essential stores); and the British losses [at Fayal], though heavy, were minute in proportion to the whole force that Cochrane employed. But Reid's action was extremely gallant and brilliant.

and passed. He and his 2,000 reinforcements didn't arrive until November, putting off the sailing of the invasion fleet until the twenty-sixth of that month. By the time the British arrived before New Orleans in December, Jackson had had enough time to rally his men.

One can only speculate as to what Jackson's political future might have been had Cochrane made his landing in the latter part of November as planned. The military significance of a British victory and occupation of New Orleans would have been minor, as the War of 1812 was already being settled at the peace tables in Europe. But the effect on the reputation of Andrew Jackson as a military leader would have been considerable.

Sam Reid and his men returned to the United States after the war and were widely acclaimed. Reid was feted at a state banquet in Richmond, Virginia, and was awarded a sword of honor by New York City. Then, his brief moment in history past, he turned to the more prosaic task of rearing a family.

But there was one more service to his country for which Reid deserves lasting recognition. Since 1795 and all through the War of 1812, American armies and ships had flown a flag of fifteen stars and fifteen stripes. Several states had joined the Union since that time, and now clamored for recognition.

Reid had long felt that the flag wasn't truly representative, and when his advice was sought by a congressional committee investigating new designs—its chairman was a personal friend—Reid was ready. He suggested that the fifteen stripes be reduced to thirteen as a permanent honor to the original thirteen colonies, and that a star be added to the existing fifteen for each new state admitted to the Union. His recommendations were accepted, and a bill embodying them was signed by President James Monroe on April 9, 1818. In honor of her husband's assistance, Mrs. Reid was given the privilege of fashioning the first flag of the new design; it flew for the first time over the Capitol on April 13.

Reid later served as New York's first harbor master and instituted such improvements as the Sandy Hook lightship and a ship-to-shore telegraph system for reporting arrivals. He ended his career in 1855—as a 72-year-old sailing master in the Navy—and died in 1861, at the beginning of the Civil War. But his greatest service to his country had been rendered in a much earlier war—on that September night in 1814 when, against terrific odds, he stood his ground and made his place in history—at a distant port called Fayal.

Wallace C. Baker of Massapequa Park, New York, is publications editor for a Long Island manufacturing concern.

THE SIEGE OF WAKE ISLAND

An eyewitness account by John R. Burroughs

For the United States forces in the Pacific, the first months of World War II were a time of unremitting disaster. Undermanned, outgunned, and hardly prepared for a struggle of such magnitude, our scattered garrisons could hope only to delay and hinder the Japanese onslaught until the nation's war machine grew strong enough to contain it. One of the most gallant of these desperate holding actions was the defense of Wake Island in December, 1941. Although tiny and remote—this 2,600-acre wishbone of sand and coral is 450 miles from the nearest land—Wake was of considerable strategic importance: for America, it was part of the defense chain that linked the Pacific Coast with the Philippines and the mainland of Asia; for the enemy it was a stepping stone toward Midway and the Hawaiian Islands. At the time of the Japanese attack, Wake was defended by 450 marines under Major James P. S. Devereux, and approximately 1,200 civilian workers, one of whom was a construction engineer named John R. Burroughs. During three and a half years of captivity in prison camps in China and Japan, Burroughs kept a record of his war experiences, which he has recently put together in book form. It is from that work that this account of the last sixteen days of Wake is taken.

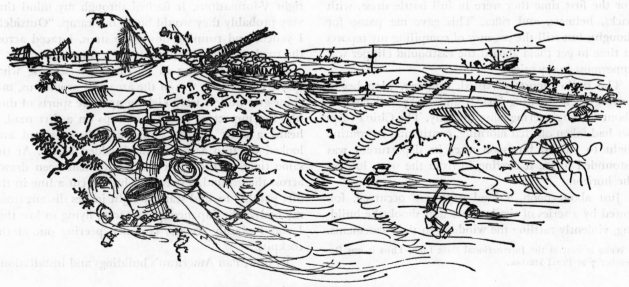

ILLUSTRATED FOR AMERICAN HERITAGE BY GIL WALKER

On Monday morning, December 8 (Wake Island time),* 1941, we reported for work at seven o'clock as usual. At about eight, my friend Bob Bryan, a clerk in the engineering office, came to my desk, greatly excited.

"There's a report coming in on the radio that the Japs have attacked Pearl Harbor, and are bombing and machine-gunning Schofield Barracks!" he exclaimed.

I heard trucks rumbling over the Peale Island bridge. (Wake Island is actually an atoll composed of three islands: Peale, Wilkes, and the largest, Wake.) Looking out of the window, I saw the usual working party of marines who were building machine-gun pits on the windward side of Peale Island pass by. For the first time they were in full battle dress, with packs, helmets, and rifles. This gave me pause for thought, but still the urgency of compiling my reports in time to get them aboard the eastbound clipper was uppermost in my mind.

The radio reports persisted, however. Men began leaving their drawing boards and desks and circling about the engineering office uneasily. The China Clipper had taken off that morning, continuing its routine flight to Guam; but soon after its departure I was astounded to see it circling in from the west, low on the horizon.

Just about noon, a loud explosion occurred, followed by a series of similar ones that shook the building, violently rattling the windows in their casements.

* Wake is west of the International Date Line. Thus it was December 7 at Pearl Harbor.

The first thought entering my mind was that the drill crews had set off some particularly heavy charges in the lagoon—for they had been at work for the past month blasting coral-heads to clear the seaplane runways. But outside, the lagoon was placid in the sunlight.

I joined a group of men from my department and from the engineering office who were running into the hall and toward the exterior door. Then for the first time I heard the drone of engines and the rapid staccato of machine-gun fire. Someone yelled, "Hit the floor!"

I crawled to the door on my hands and knees to look out. All along the water front clouds of black smoke were pouring upward; crossing the lagoon at an altitude of five or six hundred feet, headed in our direction, were three squadrons of two-engine bombers in tight V-formations. It flashed through my mind that very probably they would bomb our camp. "Outside!" I yelled, and running down the steps, I raced across the road and threw myself under a stunted tree.

Men were running in all directions seeking what sparse cover there was in the area. All around us, machine-gun bullets were kicking up little spurts of dust like the impact of heavy raindrops on a dirt road. I heard a swift tearing sound directly overhead and looked up into a shower of shredded leaves. At the same time, as though a sharp stick had been drawn across the ground, a stream of bullets cut a line in the dirt parallel to, and scarcely eight inches distant from, my body. The Japanese planes were flying so low that I could plainly see the crewmen peering out of the cockpits.

By now, Pan American's buildings and installations,

as well as many of the permanent establishments that we had built on Peale Island, were roaring infernos of flame and smoke corkscrewing into the sky. Evidently the Japanese had expended their bomb load on our land-plane runway, for they passed over our camp strafing but not bombing. After they disappeared, I stood up, feeling queer in the knees. I looked at my watch. It was twelve o'clock "straight up." From beginning to end the attack had not lasted more than four or five minutes.

I ran back into the office, grabbed the cost ledgers, shoved them in a filing cabinet, and closed and locked the drawer. Reynold Carr, one of my clerks, called, "Hey, look at this!" A bullet had drilled a neat hole through the seat of his chair. He had missed death by seconds. We found other holes in the floor and walls.

Leaving the office, I walked toward the mess hall. It being near mealtime, scores of men had been on the mall when the attack came, and yet, miraculously, none of them had been hit. Men were now scattered about in little groups, talking in hushed voices, some squatting on their heels intently digging in the ground with pocketknives in search of bullets. Williamson, the assistant steward, came out of the mess hall and climbed on a table. "There'll be no seating today," he said. "We'll serve lunch cafeteria-style. Get in line. Pass through the kitchen to get your grub, then go outside—and don't bunch up."

I gulped the food, returned the utensils to the mess hall, and crossing to my bunkhouse, hurriedly made up a bedroll. I looked at the pictures on the shelf, hesitated a moment, and decided to leave them and my other possessions where they were. Shouldering the bedroll and pocketing toothbrush, tooth powder, and some chocolate bars I had purchased at the canteen, I left. I never entered the bunkhouse again. It was bombed out of existence the following day.

My bunkhouse was situated on a side road debouching on the arterial road which led to the Peale Island bridge. As I approached the main road, I saw two trucks and a pickup crossing the bridge very slowly; I stepped aside to permit them to turn down the side road to the hospital. The truck swung around the curve, a corner of its tail gate passing within a foot of my face. Its bed was covered with wounded, dying, and dead men, sprawled on rumpled, bloody quilts. Nearest me, his head, neck, and shoulder a lacerated mass, was a man whose arm was connected to his body by the merest shred of flesh. Half of his skull had been blown away, and his brains were oozing through the jagged aperture onto the quilt. The second truck and the pickup carried the same grim cargo.

Work parties were being made up in front of the contractor's office. I remember Lieutenant Commander Elmer Greey, the Navy's resident officer in the construction camp, asking me if I was arranging transportation back home and my reply that I was scheduled to report to the Marine camp with a party of volunteers. We tossed our bedrolls onto a truck and climbed in.

Our immediate task was the decentralization of .30 and .50-caliber machine-gun ammunition. Speed was imperative. The heavy cases were stacked in great piles high under the rafters of a long, sheet-iron warehouse building. Men swarmed up these piles while those of us below formed two lines. The cases began moving out rapidly. We shoved them aboard a truck, which transported them out to the parade ground where they were unloaded and hastily buried.

Before we had completed the decentralization of the small arms ammunition, ten of us were assigned to a detail engaged in trucking three-inch antiaircraft shells from temporary frame magazines to the gun batteries. About five o'clock, we finished supplying the Wilkes Island battery, and headed in our truck for the contractor's camp. As we crossed the east-west runway of the airfield, a sad sight, formidable in its implications, met our eyes. Seven of our twelve Grumman Wildcat fighters were broken in two, their empennages and radial engines pointing skyward at sharp angles. Four of them had been set on fire by machine-gun strafing, and three were damaged beyond repair by close bomb hits. An eighth plane had been damaged but was in repairable condition.

Our Marine aviation personnel had also suffered heavy casualties. Of the pilots, First Lieutenant George Graves and Second Lieutenants Frank Holden and Robert Conderman had been killed, and Second Lieutenant Henry Webb severely wounded. The casualties had been proportionately heavy among the members of the ground crew. The loss of these pilots, as well as seven of our twelve fighter planes, on the first day of hostilities was the worst possible blow to our defenses.

All the planes had been aloft most of the morning; at the time of the attack, however, only four were up, the others having returned to base for refueling. Had the enemy delayed twenty minutes, we would have had eight planes in the sky, with two more ready to take off.

The initial success of the Japanese in taking the island by surprise can be attributed to the skill with which they made use of cloud cover. All morning the sky had been overcast, and a long dense cloud bank lay parallel to and directly above Wake's lee shore. Apparently the Japanese came in high, and while still far out to sea, cut their engines. They glided in, darting out of this cloud bank at an alti-

tude of a thousand or fifteen hundred feet, and were over our airfield before we were aware of their existence.

At ten o'clock that night I found myself a member of a crew unloading antiaircraft shells near the extremity of Peacock Point. Fred Hauner, one of the men from my department, was with me. When we had unloaded the truck, Fred and I headed down the trail toward the Five-Inch battery. A sentry challenged us. "This is Burroughs," I answered. "Where is Lieutenant Barninger?"

Sergeant Boscarino, gun captain on gun No. 1, came up. "We've fixed up foxholes for you men. That's what we were doing during the bombing. We didn't waste any time. Come on and I'll show you where they are."

Fred and I followed, stumbling in the inky blackness, our feet catching on the creeping vines.

"There it is," Boscarino said, pointing to a smudge one degree blacker than the enveloping night. There was hardly room enough for the two of us to squeeze inside the foxhole. The "floor" was covered with coral cobbles the size of a man's fist. We each had a blanket, a sheet, and a canvas bedcover. I was too exhausted to fall asleep. For a long time I lay twisting on the pernicious coral, trying to avoid the drip of the rain that had begun to fall, and listening to the ominous boom and rumble of the nearby surf.

Fred and I awoke at daybreak and crawled out of our hole. In the west, smoke still ascended from the preceding day's holocaust. We had learned that Pan Am's casualties were ten men—mostly Chamorro boys from Guam—dead, and that some thirty service men had been killed or wounded in the attack on the airport. An undetermined number of contractor's men were casualties. The hospital was full, and the contractor's surgeon, Dr. Lawton Shank, and the Navy medical officer, Lieutenant Gustave Kahn, had operated without rest all during the afternoon and night of December 8.

Fred and I went down to Battery A's range finder and passed the time of day with the marines. Boscarino quickly instructed us in the use of a .30-caliber machine gun, and showed us which foxholes we were to occupy in the event an air raid caught us while we were working around the battery. A klaxon which could be heard all over the point had been rigged up to give the alarm when enemy planes came in sight.* Lookouts equipped with binoculars were posted on the range finder shelter, and on top of Lieutenant Barninger's battery command post.

Dead tired from the excitement and the work of the preceding day, and from a sleepless, rain-drenched

* Unfortunately, Wake Island was not equipped with radar.

night, I stretched out on a rock and was nearly asleep when the klaxon sounded. As distant as the drowsy hum of bees on a sultry summer day I could hear the engines of the approaching planes. This time the Japanese did not have the advantage of a surprise attack. First I heard the rapid staccato of our .50-caliber machine guns, and then the close, loud, hollow-sounding "pung-pung-punging" as the AA battery under the command of Lieutenant William Lewis went into action. Fred and I crouched against the rear wall of our foxhole, as far back as it was possible to get from the brilliant splash of sunlight on the white rocks at the entrance.

The enemy flight was passing directly over Peacock Point. Above the ever-present pounding of the surf a new sound came to my ears: first, a swift rustling as of heavy silk; then a shrill thin scream culminating in a shattering explosion. I shrank back, instinctively throwing my arm in front of my eyes. The ground shuddered. Rock fragments were falling on the roof of our foxhole like the steady pounding of heavy rain. A rock the size of my head catapulted into the opening and rolled against my feet. As the sound of bursting bombs grew fainter and fainter, I crawled to the door and looked out.

Nearby, the leaves on the shrubbery were gray-coated with dust. Fred came out of the hole, and we stood on the rocks watching a huge conflagration in the contractor's camp. Soon all of Peale Island and the northwesternmost tip of Wake were blanketed by flame and smoke. Now and then a new wisp of light-gray smoke would rise and mingle with the black, as another frame building took fire.

We went down to the battery command post. Bit by bit, disastrous news came over the wire. The contractor's warehouse in Camp Two had been hit. Our machine shop and adjacent oil and gasoline stores had been completely wiped out. The explosive and incendiary bombs had cut a swath right through the center of the contractor's camp. The Nipponese had succeeded in bombing and burning the company hospital, which was crammed with men wounded in the preceding day's attack. I learned later that my bunkhouse had burned to the ground in this raid, leaving me bereft of all my possessions except the clothing I wore.

One fact of these raids struck me as peculiarly significant. The Japanese had carefully avoided destroying the powerhouses in the two camps, the bridge connecting Wake and Peale islands, and the nearly completed Naval Air Station barracks building on Peale. This seemed strange, for without the powerhouses, the fresh water distilleries could not be oper-

68

ated, and without the distilleries we soon would be forced to capitulate because of thirst. But it also occurred to me that perhaps the Japanese were bent not so much on our destruction and the eradication of Wake Island as an effective link in our aerial communications with the Philippines, as they were in preserving our most essential installations for themselves. Of course this meant but one thing: landing parties—an attempt to storm the island—and this posed a serious personal problem to all civilian personnel.

The marines on the island were, essentially, a working party, many of them not long out of boot camp. The first full-strength defense battalion, it was rumored, was not due to arrive until January 9, 1942. Even the servicemen on the island were under-armed. Let me emphasize that the terms of our working agreements with the contractors prohibited our bringing personal weapons to the island. Yet there we were—1,200 unarmed men—living like rats in the middle of a battlefield! A weapon in a man's hands gives him confidence. We did not have weapons. All we could do was crouch behind rocks and scoot from foxhole to foxhole.

On the morning of December 10 the raid alarm sounded about ten forty-five. This time, 26 planes came over, bombing from Peacock Point to Kuku Point, the heaviest attack having been reserved for the Marine camp, which was ablaze. The water-front oil dump also was on fire.

Just before dawn on the eleventh, I was awakened by shouting outside our foxhole. I heard my name called, and caught the words "all civilians down on the guns."

In the east the sky was slightly less black than total night. I felt the morning mist on my face. Men were emerging from the foxholes and running in the direction of Peacock Point. We followed, stumbling over the sharp coral boulders.

Lieutenant Barninger, a shadowy figure, stood upright on the roof of his command post. He was peering out to sea through his binoculars. I heard him say, "I can't make out what they are . . ." There were ships lying offshore.

Sergeant Poulousky was coming up the trail. "I want you take charge of the powder magazine," he said quickly. "Come along." The magazine looked exactly like a big vine-covered coral boulder. In reality the "boulder" was a large tarpaulin stretched over a wooden framework; under this camouflage a rectangle of sandbags outlined a trap door at ground level. We raised the trap door and propped it open. "Watch your head," Poulousky said.

"The shells are on this side," he explained, "and the powder canisters over here. See these shells?" He took my hand and guided it to several shells standing in a vertical position on the floor. "There's nine star shells here. For God's sake don't send *them* up."

I straightened up, bumping my head.

"If we go into action," Poulousky continued, "pass up two shells—one for each gun. Then two powders—understand?"

I followed him back up the ladder. Johnny Clelan and several other civilians were grouped about the entrance.

Poulousky turned to Clelan. "If we go into action, you stand at the head of the ladder here and take the stuff from Burroughs. Send a powder and a shell to gun No. 1, then a powder and a shell to gun No. 2—keep alternating."

We squatted around the magazine on our haunches talking in low tones about what might be "out there." We had heard that contractor's personnel on Johnston, Palmyra, and Midway islands had been evacuated several days previously. Thus we were inclined to think that the ships offshore had brought reinforcements, and, happiest thought of all, probably there would be

an aircraft carrier in the flotilla. This optimistic trend of thought was shattered abruptly by Lieutenant Barninger's steady voice: "There's a red ball on her funnel."

Poulousky came tearing from the brush, yelling: "All right, you civilians, break out those shells . . ." I dived down the ladder and fumbled for the first tier in the darkness. I grasped a shell. Johnny Clelan was crouching in the aperture above. I heaved upward, first a shell, then a powder canister. I could hear Tony Poulousky shouting excitedly: "Come on, you God-damned civilians, hurry up with those shells"; heard the heavy breathing of the men, and the sound of running feet on the coral.

"Okay down there," Poulousky yelled, "we've got enough stuff on top. Come up for a breather."

I climbed up the ladder, lifted the canvas, and crawling outside, sat down on a rock. A series of long flashes far out at sea lightened the horizon. Seconds later a sound like distant thunder reached my ears. Suddenly flames, followed by a thick column of black smoke, arose in the vicinity of the marines' camp.

The sky was light now, and I could distinguish the outlines of three ships inshore from the horizon. Following closely on the flashes from the enemy guns, I heard Lieutenant Barninger's voice: "Range four thousand . . ." He was  squatting on his heels, binoculars intent on the target, and his voice calling the range came easily. Major Potter, commanding the five-inch gun positions, wisely had given orders to the battery commanders to hold their fire until the Japanese were close in.

Our initial target was a light cruiser broadside to us. The first shot from our gun No. 1 fell far short due to defective range setting, whereas gun No. 2 overshot the target; we were without electrical or compressed air control, and the gun captains were firing by lanyard. On the second salvo both guns fell short; the ship was moving out. Then, methodically, our battery built up to the target until, eight or ten minutes after we had gone into action, we scored a direct hit at a range of about 7,000 yards. It struck square amidship and right at the water line.

First a wisp of white emanated from the warship, followed by a big puff of steam. Brown smoke began billowing from her belly.*

From the smoke rising over the island, I could tell that the Japanese bombardment had set more of our

* Lieutenant Barninger's battery had hit the light cruiser *Yubari*, flagship of the Japanese invasion force.

oil tanks afire. Opposite the entrance to the small boat channel between Wake and Wilkes, a transport was hastily drawing off in flames. Far out at sea a small ship had been hit and seemed to be sinking.

The east was crimson and orange now, the earth-curve etched against the sky by the rolling Pacific. Each enemy unit stood clearly limned in the new light. Just beyond the transport, a smaller warship was falling apart.

I heard Lieutenant Barninger say: "They're drawing off . . ." Then: "Range 17,500!" A thrill of enthusiasm ran through me. The Japanese had attacked in considerable strength—there had been at least two cruisers, four or five destroyers, and several auxiliary craft in their flotilla, with a possible fire-power of fifty or sixty naval rifles running up to ten- or twelve-inch caliber available against us—and we had beaten them off with three batteries of five-inch guns!

One of those freakish happenings that sometimes occur in battle chalked up an additional warship for Lieutenant Barninger's battery. From our position we were unable to see a Japanese destroyer lying beyond, but in the same azimuth as the cruiser at which we were firing. At his command post down on the reef, Lieutenant Robert M. Hanna could see this destroyer, however. He told me that the first shot fired from our gun No. 2, which overreached the cruiser, plopped squarely into this destroyer.

In their overconfidence the Japanese had walked into a trap, heaving-to to send in and to cover landing parties within a triangle formed by our land batteries and an American submarine which lay hidden on their seaward side. Our aviators, too, had scored heavily, ferrying bombs with which they smeared the enemy throughout the engagement. Except for the burning of tanks, the Japanese guns had done little damage. From the first shot to the last, not more than an hour had elapsed. For some time smoke and flames still were visible far at sea mingling with the heavy white smoke screen thrown out by their remaining destroyers.*

I put the magazine in order and then walked down to the range finder. The men in the range section were jubilant. Sergeant Boscarino came up from his gun. His face was grimed and black with powder smoke. He still wore the protective pad on his left forearm with which he wiped the "mushroom" on the breechblock after each round had been fired. Everyone congratulated each other.

* In the engagement of December 11, the Wake Island shore batteries sank one Japanese destroyer and badly damaged several other warships. Thirty miles southwest of the atoll, the Grumman fighters sank a second destroyer. It was the last time in the Pacific War that coast defense guns repelled an amphibious landing. —Ed.

At nine thirty the next morning, the Japanese raided Wake Island again. There seemed to be more planes than usual—I learned later that thirty bombers had come over—but they dropped fewer bombs. When they had passed over, I ventured out of the foxhole. Our few planes already were in the sky, and were diving into the enemy formations. The AA batteries on Peacock Point and on Peale Island opened up. The shells burst high in the sky, leaving white puffs intermingled with the tiny birdlike specks that were the enemy planes. Our few Grummans buzzed in and out of the enemy formations like hornets, oftentimes following the Japanese bombers amid the bursts of our own anti-aircraft fire.

One evening shortly after the sea attack, I went down to the water to bathe. Lying on my back in a shallow pool, and listening to the pounding of the surf on the outlying reef, I felt perfectly safe. So far all air raids had come in the forenoon, and we had arrived at the conclusion that the Japanese planes—which, we presumed, were coming from the Marshall Islands, some six hundred miles to the south—found it inexpedient to return to their bases after nightfall.

I had come out of the water and was reaching for my towel when I heard someone shout. Looking up, I saw two marines running full tilt along the shore. It suddenly occurred to me that I was upwind from the range finder, and very possibly had missed the air raid alarm. Even with this thought I heard the sound of engines rising above the roar of the sea. I jerked on my shoes, snatched up my clothing, and ran for cover. As the first bombs fell, I scrambled into our foxhole, stark naked. It was a rather close call, but I had put on a good show for the other boys, and the explosion of the bombs was punctuated by their laughter.

Day followed day. There was no telling now when the Nipponese air arm would strike. Sometimes the klaxon awakened us at dawn. Again it sounded in the mid or late afternoon. Sometimes the enemy attacked twice in the same day; and as time wore on, one question loomed in the minds of civilians and servicemen alike: "Where, in Christ's name, was the U. S. Navy?" When would our people send reinforcements?

Life had been reduced to its simplest elements: we ate when food was available, slept, bathed infrequently, answered our nature calls. This life was lived in an atmosphere of ever-increasing apprehension. The feeling of exhilaration arising from our success in the battle of December 11 had worn off. The air raids continued. Though casualties were slight, and little damage was done, the damnable persistence of the Japanese had the effect of disrupting any attempts at large-scale reorganization for effective defense work.

Late on the afternoon of December 20, a United States PBY flying boat arrived at Wake Island. Word reached us over the grapevine that it had come for the purpose of delivering sealed orders to Commander Winfield Cunningham, who was in charge of the small naval detachment on the island.

The insouciance of the three aviators, their ignorance regarding the plight we were in, and their nonchalant request to be conducted to the Pan American Hotel, left us a little flabbergasted and vastly discouraged.

The PBY took off on the return trip at seven o'clock the following morning carrying Major Baylor, USMC, as a passenger. He was the last man to get away from the island. Two days later we were prisoners of the Japanese.

At eight fifty A.M. the inevitable alarm sounded. It was only a matter of seconds until we realized that this was no ordinary raid: the nerve-shattering roaring of the engines close overhead was exceeded only by the repetitive swish and scream and crashing crescendo of the falling bombs. Each ear-splitting detonation shook the timbers in our dugout. There was no surcease, no breathing spell between explosions.

Dive bombers were unloading their cargoes on us in sticks of four. Dropped at water's edge, the fourth bomb to fall was intended for the Peacock Point installations. We would hear the explosions of bombs one, two, and three, and then, when our turn came, the beams rattled and shook, the earth trembled, and dirt and gravel sifted down on us while we lay stiff with fear.

Lieutenant Barninger was worried. The presence of the dive bombers using heavy bombs indicated that an aircraft carrier was in the vicinity, and the presence of a carrier only too clearly signified the presence of a considerable enemy flotilla.

The following day, December 22, the dive-bombing started at twelve thirty-five and lasted for forty minutes. Evidently the Nipponese had our gun positions, for they hit Peacock Point hard. A large-caliber bomb had hit within twenty feet of gun No. 2's dugout, and nineteen marines had been pinned against the wall by heavy timbers. Had the concussion been a trifle heavier, all of them would have been crushed to death.

Our last two planes, piloted by Captain Herbert Freuler and Lieutenant Carl Davidson, went into the air that morning to meet the dive bombers coming in from the sea. There was dogfighting all over the sky.

After destroying one Japanese plane Captain Freuler looked up in time to see another coming at him intent on *kamikaze*. He gave it a burst of bullets, jerked back on the stick, and zoomed upward, barely avoiding a head-on collision. As he passed over, the enemy plane blew up. The force of the explosion stunned Freuler. Looking down he saw fragments of the disintegrated plane splashing all over the lagoon. A third plane was coming in on his tail. The force of the explosion had loosened the fabric on the ailerons and stabilizers, and Freuler's plane responded to the controls sluggishly. Before he could pull away, the Japanese flier had him. Badly wounded, he put his Grumman into a sideslip and made for the airport. His plane was behaving erratically. He made a pass at the field, but the Jap bombers were working it over and there was no chance to land. He made a wide circle and again came in. By this time he had lost a great deal of blood, and was weakening rapidly and feeling faint. Finally, on the fourth pass, he managed to set his plane down on the field. A fellow pilot, who was at the airport at the time, described Freuler's condition:

We found him slumped unconscious in a pool of blood, a big chink shot out of the flesh of his shoulder. Another bullet had penetrated the gas tank, pierced the back of the seat, the folded parachute pack, Freuler's clothing, and lodged against his spine. We found a .60 caliber slug in the engine. The oil-line was cut. The fabric of the controls was lying in folds. Everything—Freuler, the motor, the plane— "conked out" at the same time!

Lieutenant Carl Davidson was the last American pilot in the air over Wake Island. He chased an enemy plane out to sea and did not return.

On the gun positions the marines were grim and silent. This sort of thing could not go on indefinitely. Everyone sensed the coming of a crisis.

The decisive action at Wake Island began shortly after one o'clock on the morning of December 23. I was awakened by Lieutenant Barninger's runner, Jesse Nowlin. I pulled on my shoes, hastened outside, and roused the civilians in the adjacent foxholes. All along the water front on the lee side of Wake and Wilkes islands, ascending red flares described graceful arcs

against the Stygian background. At sea, completely encircling the island, searchlights were at work, flash succeeding rapid flash, the long streamers of light cutting the sky into angular black chunks as the ships busily signalled to each other. Suddenly the entire beach on our side of the island was momentarily bathed in white light. This was from one of our own searchlights. It went out as suddenly as it had come on. From all directions came the clamor of machine guns, periodically punctuated by the hollow sound of our three-inch guns. From the powder magazine on Peacock Point we were unable in the darkness to make out any of the targets which attracted this voluminous fire. The number of red flares increased.

They came closer and closer, breaking over the island in ragged lines, bathing it in an eerie crimson glow. The sky now was a mosaic fashioned by tangled searchlight beams. The firing increased to a steady drumming sound. The .50-caliber nests nearby on the windward side of Peacock Point opened up. Bullets zinged close overhead, and we ducked for cover behind the sandbags protecting the magazine.

At the time the final attack came, approximately 450 servicemen were available to defend the island. These men had been on the alert at battle stations for fifteen consecutive days and nights without relief. With the exception of the plane which Captain Freuler had piloted on the afternoon of the twenty-second, and which, while repairable, would be out of commission for several days, we had lost all of our small squadron of airplanes.

As nearly as we could ascertain, the Nipponese were attempting to land all along the lee shores of Wake and Wilkes islands in motor-driven barges and boats. Throughout the night, flares also were seen over the lagoon. On Peale Island shortly before 2 A.M. the gun crews were ordered to take small arms and stand by to repel a possible landing sortie from the lagoon side. Except for reconnaissance patrols in their area, the troops on Peale Island were inactive until seven o'clock on the morning of the twenty-third when they

mand post that no crew was available to man this gun. Although he was a machine-gun specialist, Hanna asked for and obtained permission to man the three-inch gun himself. Assisted only by civilians Robert M. Bryan and Paul Gay, who had been trained on machine guns and who knew absolutely nothing about the operation of a three-inch gun, Hanna got busy.

It was pitch black and everything had to be done by "feel." Hanna told Bryan to bring the gun to bear on the target—a shadowy hulk close in, and approximately a hundred yards upshore from his position—while he proceeded to cut the fuses on several shells, making them as short as possible for a two-second burst.

Hanna loaded the three-inch piece, attached the lanyard and fired. The first shot went high. In laying the piece on the target, Bryan had sighted along the top of the barrel as one sights a shotgun or a sporting rifle. Hanna quickly lowered the muzzle and "bore-sighted" the gun. The next shot took effect.

Hanna could not recognize the nature of the target —whether it was a landing barge, a longboat or what. As its stern receded into the blackness of the night and the Pacific, he put two more shots into her. The Japanese aboard the craft, probably to give their shock troops a brief glimpse of the terrain ashore, then did a foolish thing. Momentarily they turned on a hooded spotlight on the ship's bow. It was enough. For an instant the entire structure—it was a patrol craft—was silhouetted. Hanna quickly swung the muzzle of his gun to the left. A shot—there was a muffled roar—and clouds of steam rose upward. A second shot found the ship's magazine and she went up: small-arms ammunition covered the sky with red traceries; larger shells exploded making exquisite red and white flower pots; grenades feathered out like sparklers.

The "show" was visible all over the island. By its light Hanna discovered a second ship of the same class in the immediate vicinity, and succeeded in putting several shots into her. In the haste with which it had been placed, the platform of the gun he was firing had not been seated firmly on the ground, but rested in part on some tough, springy ironwood brush. Each time it was fired, the gun jumped about like an unruly mustang, and it was necessary to check the aim before again firing. The position was exposed, and Hanna and his crew were utterly without sandbags or any other type of protection.

Dawn found twelve men defending the beach in the vicinity of Hanna's position: Hanna, Bryan, Gay, Major Putnam, Corporal John Painter, who had given an excellent account of himself as a mechanic on the airport, Marines L. V. Murphy and Baumgardner, civilians Eric

were transferred to Wake Island to join a skirmish line protecting the command post.

On Wilkes Island, however, it was a different story. Throughout the night, flares burst over the island and our machine guns fired constantly. In bombing Wilkes Island on December 10 the Japanese had hit a big cache of dynamite. The force of the terrific explosion damaged the big searchlight unit concealed in the brush nearby to such an extent that it went out of order after only a few seconds of use on the morning of the twenty-third. Consequently the defense against the landing parties was undertaken in total darkness.

The fighting on Wake Island was widespread, extending from the small boat channel eastward along the lee shore to within 150 yards of our Peacock Point positions, taking in the airport, and extending as far north as the communication center. The best way to tell the story of the melee on the lee shore of Wake, and in the brush between the road and the airport, is to relate the amazing exploit of Lieutenant Bob Hanna.

Lieutenant Hanna, being the American farthest out on the beach, was the first to discern the shadowy shapes of the Japanese landing craft silently gliding shoreward. A crew was to have been formed to service the nearby three-inch gun, but they had not arrived. Hanna got on the phone and was informed from com-

Lehtola and J. C. Smith, and three other civilians whose names are not available. Bryan was manning a .30-caliber machine gun. In addition, the party was armed with a Thompson submachine gun, a Browning automatic rifle, Springfields, and a few side arms.

Early in the war our draglines had gouged deep recesses into the bank paralleling the south side of the east-west runway for the protection of our planes when they were on the ground. Under the cover of darkness, a number of Japanese had infiltrated into these recesses, and when dawn came they gave Hanna's embattled group plenty of trouble with manually operated grenade throwers. These small mechanical mortars, with a very high trajectory, were surprisingly accurate.

Across the road from Hanna's party, in a narrow strip of brush paralleling the runway, Captain Frank Tharin and Captain Elrod were in charge of another group of skirmishers, their personnel including civilian mechanics Yeager, Gibbons, Gibbons' son, the contractor's structural steel superintendent, Pete Sorenson, and a structural steel foreman named L. H. Peterson. This patch of brush was full of Japanese and the fighting was at close quarters. Men maneuvered an inch at a time to get a shot at the Japs lying behind rocks and brush not more than twenty or twenty-five feet from them.

Hanna's party tried several times to abandon their exposed beach position and join Tharin's group in the brush, but were prevented from doing so by a Japanese machine gunner who commanded a full view of the open road which they must cross. Sorenson and Peterson, the first armed with a tommy gun, the second with a Springfield rifle, crouched behind an overturned AA carrier about fifty yards from Hanna. They too were practically in the open. They were kneeling about six or seven feet apart, when a grenade burst directly between them. By some strange freak of fortune neither man was injured. They separated, and within seconds the Jap mortars on the airport scored direct hits on each man, killing them instantly.

Bryan did yeoman service with his machine gun before a bullet pierced his forehead. Gay was killed by a machine gun burst which raked his chest, and an almost simultaneous grenade hit which practically disemboweled him. Hanna saw a Japanese firing at Major Putnam at close range. The bullet hit a three-inch shell and ricocheted harmlessly. Before the Jap could fire again, Hanna had dropped him with his .45.

In the brush across the road, Captain Elrod and young Gibbons had been killed. Captain Tharin and a companion ensconced in a bomb crater, each with a Thompson submachine gun, were having a wonderful time. A fringe of Japanese faces peered above the crater's rim—a spraying motion of the tommy guns—and the faces disappeared. When the surrender came, Tharin's foxhole literally was ringed by dozens of Japanese dead.

Just how the Japanese flanked our Wake Island positions is not entirely clear. Evidently under cover of darkness they entered the lagoon over the reef in rubber boats and secreted themselves in the thick brush along the lagoon side of Wake Island. Men attached to Lieutenant Lewis' AA battery reported that early in the morning they were fired on from that direction. After the surrender, a Japanese officer told one of the contractor's engineers whom he had put to work straightening out blueprints in the office, that further resistance on our part would have proven futile in any event; that there were over 150 Japanese naval vessels within an hour's call of Wake Island that morning.

The island was surrendered unconditionally about eight o'clock on the morning of December 23, a few hours less than sixteen days after the Japanese launched their first attack from the air.

It is interesting to know that the Japanese landing parties were a long way from defeating the American garrison in the field. Actually, throughout the early morning hours, we had them beaten. The main American skirmish line defending the command post, ex-

tending across Wake Island from the lagoon to Windy Beach, never did engage the enemy. On the lee shore of Wake, the parties commanded by Captain Tharin and Major Putnam were holding their own, and on Wilkes Island the force under Captain Platt had completely eliminated the attackers.

Practically alone in the command post, throughout the early hours of the morning of December 23 Major Devereux received reports from his officers in the field regarding enemy strength. Fifty to a hundred planes of all classes were in sight, and estimates of enemy vessels offshore ranged from sixteen to twenty-five or thirty with, undoubtedly, other units lying out of sight beyond the horizon.

In view of enemy strength, the ultimate outcome of the engagement was not in doubt. The opinion of the Marine officers and noncommissioned officers was that we would have been able to withstand the Japanese attacks throughout the day of the twenty-third, but that they would have overrun the island the following night under conditions that would have made formal surrender impossible.

In my estimation Commander Cunningham and Major Devereux showed rare good judgment, and saved the lives of the men on the island, by timing the surrender when they did. No doubt a sense of responsibility toward us civilians was a factor figuring in the capitulation.

Throughout the night, nine of us civilians on Peacock Point had lain under the camouflage on top of the trap door to Battery A's powder magazine, squeezed between the sandbags for protection from the bullets streaming overhead. With the first faint glimmer of daylight, enemy planes, coming in low, swooped over our position. Retreat to the dugout was impossible; for all we knew, our battery might go into action at any moment, in which event we would be needed.

There was only one thing to do. Hastily we raised the trap door and the nine of us tumbled into the magazine, where we crouched between the tiered powder canisters and the racks of shells.

Time passed. The sky lightened. The steady drumming of machine guns came from all sides. I looked through the small screened vent at ground level and was surprised to see the long tube of our gun No. 1 stripped of camouflage, ready for action. None of the marines was in sight. Fortunately for us unarmed civilians, the Japanese landing parties avoided the strong rip-tides off Peacock Point, and passed a hundred yards to the west of our position on their way to the airport.

The sun was up now. A plane dived directly on us, passed close—scarcely a hundred feet overhead—and,

miracle of miracles, nothing happened. Then we noticed a significant lull in the firing of the machine guns. I risked a glimpse top-side. Overhead a multitude of planes of all types were flying low over the island. Our two naval rifles, stripped of their camouflage, were naked and cold-looking in the early morning sunlight. They were glaring targets, but the Japanese airmen ignored them. I couldn't figure it out.

After the hours of incessant gun fire, the sudden absolute quiet was awesome. We whispered in muted tones, or kept quiet, admonishing others to do likewise by sign language. Except for the soft murmur of a quiet sea lapping at the coral pebbles on the beach, Peacock Point was absolutely still.

At long last a man appeared in the clearing in the rear of our guns. It was Sergeant Warren. Approaching the magazine, he called: "You people can come on up. It's all over. The island's surrendered."

I don't know just what I did expect, but I hadn't expected *that*. The thing that must not happen, the thing we dreaded most—more than mutilation or death—had happened. In a benumbed state of mind, I automatically took out the small notebook in which I had been keeping a diary, tore it into small fragments, and scattered them among the powder canisters. Loosening my belt, I removed the only weapon I possessed—a clasp knife with a four-inch blade—and tossed it behind a rack of shells. I crawled outside, and, unutterably weary, stood on unsteady legs.

Slowly, we made our way to the range finder. The skirmish line had broken up, and men were coming out of the brush from all directions. Some of the marines were busy opening tinned food. "Eat all you can," Lieutenant Barninger admonished, "it may be a long time to the next meal." He turned toward us. "You civilians get away from the battery. The Japs may class you as guerrillas if they find you here."

"Let's go up on the road and see what it's all about," I said to Johnny Clelan.

Johnny and I shook hands all around with the marines, and started up the trail. We came out on the road, and walked in the direction of the contractor's camp.

The rounded dirt-covered crests of the four high-explosive magazines loomed ahead. A Japanese flag floated on top of one of them. Someone had left a half-full number ten can of pineapple rings in the middle of the road. We hooked several rings of the fruit over our fingers and walked toward captivity eating nonchalantly.

Two Japanese soldiers were standing on either side of the road in front of the first of the magazines. My initial impression of them was that they carried unusually long rifles and bayonets. A second glance revealed that the rifles were of ordinary size, but that the men holding them were very small. Both were wearing split-toed sneakers, which gave them a cloven-hoofed appearance. Round canvas-covered helmets came low over their heads and necks.

Beyond the sentries, a considerable group of nearly naked Americans were lying or sitting in the middle of the road. As we approached, the sentries grunted, making upward thrusts with their bayonets. We raised our hands over our heads. One of them stepped forward and pulled at my shirt, pointing at a heap of clothing by the side of the road. We stripped down, being allowed to retain only our under-shorts, socks, and shoes. Then we were herded in with the other prisoners, most of whom were trussed up with telephone wire cut from nearby communication lines. Their legs were tied together at the ankles. Their crossed wrists had been tied and drawn up between their shoulder blades, the lashings then looped around their throats in such a manner that any effort to release their wrists, or to relieve their arms from the twisted, cramped position, automatically resulted in cutting off their wind—an ingenious lash-up which rendered them perfectly inert. Many men wore dirty, blood-soaked bandages.

Japanese sentries with fixed bayonets stood guard over us. On top of a nearby high-explosive magazine, a sailor trained a light machine gun in our direction. The Japs were highly elated. Planes roared overhead. One of them—a biplane with pontoons—meandered over at an altitude of forty or fifty feet. The sailor on the magazine stood up, yelled "*banzai*," and waved his cap.

I looked out to sea. Hard by the reef, standing so close to each other that it seemed the bow of one overlapped the stern of the other, rising and falling with the ocean swells, Japanese men-of-war completely ringed the island. Not until years later, after V-J day, in fact, when I flew over Yokohama harbor en route to Guam, did I see so many ships assembled.

and exhorting, "with all possible energy and ecstasy."

That broke the dam. The sinners of Red River had spent a lonely winter with pent-up terrors gnawing at them. McGee's appeal was irresistible. In a moment the floor was "covered with the slain; their screams for mercy pierced the heavens." Cursers, duelers, whiskey-swillers, and cardplayers lay next to little children of ten and eleven, rolling and crying in "agonies of distress" for salvation. It was a remarkable performance for a region "destitute of religion." When it was through, a new harvest of souls had been gathered for the Lord.

Word of the Red River meeting whisked through the territory. When McGready got to Muddy River, his next congregation, new scenes of excitement were enacted. During the meeting, sinners prayed and cried for mercy once again, and some of them, overwhelmed by feeling, bolted from the house and rushed in agony into the woods. Their cries and sobs could be heard ringing through the surrounding trees. And when this meeting had yielded up its quota of saved, the Kentucky Revival was not only a fact, but a well-known one. McGready announced another sacramental meeting for Gasper River, and before long, dozens, perhaps hundreds, of Kentuckians who did not belong to his district were threading the trails on their way to the service. Some came as far as a hundred miles, a hard week's trip in the back country. In wagons, on horseback, and on foot came the leather-shirted men, rifles balanced on their shoulders, and their pinched-looking, tired women, all looking for blessed assurance and a washing away of their sins.

At Gasper River, history was made. The cabins of the neighborhood could not hold the influx of visitors, so the newcomers came prepared to camp out. They brought tents—some of them—and cold pork, roasted hens, slabs of corn bread, and perhaps a little whiskey to hold them up through the rigors of a long vigil. The Gasper River meetinghouse was too small for the crowd, so the men got out their educated axes, and in a while the clop-clop of tree-felling formed an overture to the services. Split-log benches were dragged into place outdoors, and the worshipers adjourned to God's first temple. What was taking place was an outdoor religious exercise, meant to last two or three days, among people who camped on the spot. This was the camp meeting. Some claimed that Gasper River sheltered the very first of them. That claim has been challenged in the court of historical inquiry. But whether it stands up or not, the Gasper River meeting

was something new in worship. It took its form from its western surroundings. Outsiders were a long time in understanding it, because they saw its crude outside and not its passionate heart.

The outside was raw enough. Once again McGready exhorted, and once again sinners fell prostrate to the ground. Night came on; inside the meetinghouse, candlelight threw grotesque, waving shadows on the walls. Outside, the darkness deepened the sense of mystery and of eternity's nearness. Preachers grew hoarse and exhausted, but insatiable worshipers gathered in knots to pray together, and to relieve their feelings by telling each other of "the sweet wonders which they saw in Christ." Hour followed hour, into dawn. For people who had to rise (and generally retire) with the sun each day of their lives, this alone was enough to make the meeting memorable for the rest of their lives. Lightheaded and hollow-eyed, the "mourners," or unconverted, listened alternately to threats of sulphur and promises of bliss, from Saturday until Monday. On Tuesday, after three throbbing days, they broke it up. Forty-five had professed salvation. Satan had gotten a thorough gouging.

Now the tide of camp-meeting revivalism began to roll northward. One of the visitors at the Logan County meetings was a young Presbyterian clergyman whose life was something of a copy of McGready's. Barton Warren Stone too had learned on the frontier to revere God Almighty and to farm well. He too had studied religion in a log college. But more than this, he was one of McGready's own converts, having fallen under the power of the older man's oratory in North Carolina. Stone liked what he observed in Logan County, and he took McGready's preaching methods and the camp-meeting idea back to his own congregations in Bourbon County, well to the north and east. Soon he too had imitators, among them Richard McNemar, who had small Presbyterian charges across the river in Ohio.

But it was Stone himself who touched off the monster camp meeting of the region's history. He set a sacramental service for August 6, 1801, at Cane Ridge, not far from the city of Lexington. Some undefinable current of excitement running from cabin to cabin brought out every Kentuckian who could drop his earthly concerns and move, by horseflesh or shoe leather, towards the campground. Later on, some people estimated that 25,000 were on hand, but that figure is almost too fantastic for belief. In 1800, Kentucky had only a quarter of a million residents, and Lexington, the largest town, numbered under two thousand. But even a crowd of three or four thousand would have overwhelmed anything in the previous experience of the settlers.

Whatever the actual number, there was a sight to dazzle the eyes of the ministers who had come. Technically the meeting was Presbyterian, but Baptist and Methodist parsons had come along, and there was room for them, because no one man could hope to reach such a mob. Preaching stands built of logs were set up outdoors. One man remembered a typical scene —a crowd spilling out of the doors of the one meeting-house, where two Presbyterian ministers were alternately holding forth, and three other groups scattered within a radius of a hundred yards. One cluster of sinners was gathered at the feet of a Presbyterian preacher, another gave ear to a Methodist exhorter, and lastly, a knot of Negroes was attending on the words of some orator of their own race. All over the campground, individual speakers had gathered little audiences to hear of *their* experiences. One observer said that there were as many as three hundred of these laymen "testifying."

So Cane Ridge was not really a meeting, but a series of meetings that gathered and broke up without any recognizable order. One Methodist brother who could not find a free preaching-stand ventured up the slanting trunk of a partly fallen tree. He found a flat spot, fifteen feet off the ground, and he spoke from this vantage point while a friend on the ground held up an umbrella on a long pole to shelter him from the weather. Within a few moments, this clergyman claimed, he had gathered an audience of thousands. Undoubtedly they stayed until lured away by some fresh address from a stump or the tail of a wagon. For the crowds were without form as they collected, listened, shouted "Amen!" and "Hallelujah!" and drifted off to find neighbors or refreshments or more preaching. The din can only be guessed at. The guilty were groaning and sometimes screaming at the top of their lungs, and those who felt that they were saved were clapping their hands, shouting hymns, and generally noising out their exultation. There were always hecklers at the meetings too, and some of them were no doubt shouting irreverent remarks at the faithful. Crying children added their bit, and tethered horses and oxen stamped, bawled, and whinnied to make the dissonance complete. Someone said that the meeting sounded from afar like the roar of Niagara. At night the campfires threw weird shadow-patterns of trees across the scene, and the whole moving, resounding  gathering appeared to be tossing on the waves of some invisible storm. As if to etch the experience into men's memories, there were real rainstorms, and the drenched participants were thrown into fresh waves of screaming as thunder and lightning crashed around them.

All in all, a memorable enough episode. And yet still stranger things happened to put the brand of the Lord's sponsorship on Cane Ridge's mass excitement. Overwhelmed with their sensations, some men and women lay rigid and stiff on the ground for hours in a kind of catalepsy. One "blasphemer" who had come to scoff at the proceedings tumbled from his saddle unconscious and remained so for a day and a half. There was something incredibly compelling in what was going on. One remembered testimony came from a reasonably hardheaded young man named James Finley. Later in life Finley became a Methodist preacher, but in 1801 he was, except for a better-than-average education, a typical frontiersman. He had a small farm, a new wife, and a vigorous love of hunting. He had come to the Cane Ridge meeting out of curiosity, but as he looked on, he was taken with an uncontrollable trembling and feelings of suffocation. He left the campground, found a log tavern, and put away a glass of brandy to steady his nerves. But they were beyond steadying. All the way home he kept breaking out in irrational fits of laughter or tears. Many a spirit, returning from Cane Ridge, must have been moved in the same near-hysterical way.

A holy frenzy seemed to have taken hold of the West. Throughout the frontier communities, the ecstasy of conversion overflowed into the nervous system. At Cane Ridge, and at a hundred subsequent meetings, the worshipers behaved in ways that would be unbelievable if there were not plenty of good testimony to their truth. Some got the "jerks," a spasmodic twitching of the entire body. They were a fearful thing to behold. Some victims hopped from place to place like bouncing balls. Sometimes heads snapped from side to side so rapidly that faces became a blur, and handkerchiefs whipped off women's heads. One preacher saw women taken with the jerks at table, so that teacups went flying from their hands to splash against log walls. Churchmen disagreed about the meaning of these symptoms. Were they signs of conversion? Or demonstrations of the Lord's power, meant to convince doubters? Peter Cartwright, a famous evangelist of a slightly later era, believed the latter. He told of a skeptic at one of his meetings who was taken with the jerks and in a particularly vicious spasm snapped his neck. He died, a witness to the judgment of Omnipotence but gasping out to the last his "cursing and bitterness." Besides the jerks, there were strange seizures in which those at prayer broke into uncontrollable guffaws or intoned weird and wordless melodies or barked like dogs.

It was wild and shaggy, and very much a part of life in the clearings. Westerners wanted to feel religion in their bones. In their tough and violent lives intellectual exercises had no place, but howls and leaps were something that men who were "half-horse and half-alligator" understood. It was natural for the frontier to get religion with a mighty roar. Any other way would not have seemed homelike to people who, half in fun and half in sheer defensiveness, loved their brag, bluster, and bluff.

Yet there was something deeper than mere excitement underneath it all. Something fundamental was taking place, some kind of genuine religious revolution, bearing a made-in-America stamp. The East was unhappy with it. For one thing, camp-meeting wildness grated on the nerves of the educated clergy. All of this jigging and howling looked more like the work of Satan than of God. There were ugly rumors, too, about unsanctified activities at the meetings. Some candidates for salvation showed up with cigars between their teeth. Despite official condemnation, liquor flowed free and white-hot on the outskirts of the gatherings. It might be that corn did more than its share in justifying God's ways to man. Then there were stories that would not down which told how, in the shadows around the clearing, excited men and women were carried away in the hysteria and, as the catch phrase had it, "begot more souls than were saved" at the meeting. All these tales might have had some partial truth, yet in themselves they did not prove much about frontier religion. As it happened, a part of every camp-meeting audience apparently consisted of loafers and rowdies who came for the show and who were quite capable of any sin that a Presbyterian college graduate was likely to imagine.

Yet it was not the unscrubbed vigor of the meetings that really bothered conservatives in the Presbyterian Church. Their fundamental problem was in adjusting themselves and their faith to a new kind of democratic urge. Enemies of the revivals did not like the success of emotional preaching. What would happen to learning, and all that learning stood for, if a leather-lunged countryman with a gift for lurid word pictures could be a champion salvationist? And what would happen—what *had* happened—to the doctrine of election when the revival preacher shouted "Repent!" at overwrought thousands, seeming to say that any Tom, Dick, or Harry who felt moved by the Spirit might be receiving the promise of eternal bliss? Would mob enthusiasm replace God's careful winnowing of the

flock to choose His lambs? The whole orderly scheme of life on earth, symbolized by a powerful church, an educated ministry, and a strait and narrow gate of salvation, stood in peril.

Nor were the conservatives wrong. In truth, when the McGreadys and Stones struck at "deadness" and "mechanical worship" in the older churches, they were going beyond theology. They were hitting out at a view of things that gave a plain and unlettered man little chance for a say in spiritual affairs. A church run by skilled theologians was apt to set rules that puzzled simple minds. A church which held that many were called, but few chosen, *was* aristocratic in a sense. The congregations of the western evangelists did not care for rules, particularly rules that were not immediately plain to anyone. In their view, the Bible alone was straightforward enough. Neither would they stand for anything resembling aristocracy, whatever form it might take. They wanted cheap land and the vote, and they were getting these things. They wanted salvation as well—or at least free and easy access to it—and they were bound to have that too. If longer-established congregations and their leaders back east did not like that notion, the time for a parting of the ways was at hand. In politics, such a parting is known as a revolution; in religion, it is schism. Neither word frightened the western revivalists very much.

The trouble did not take long to develop. In Mc-Gready's territory, a new Cumberland Presbytery, or subgroup, was organized in 1801. Before long it was in a battle with the Kentucky Synod, the next highest administrative body in the hierarchy. The specific issue was the licensing of certain "uneducated" candidates for the ministry. The root question was revivalism. The battle finally went up to the General Assembly, for Presbyterians a sort of combined Congress and Supreme Court. In 1809 the offending revivalistic presbytery was dissolved. Promptly, most of its congregations banded themselves into the separate Cumberland Presbyterian Church. Meanwhile, Barton Stone, Richard McNemar, and other members of the northern Kentucky wing of camp-meeting Presbyterianism were also in trouble. They founded a splinter group known as the "New Lights," and the Kentucky Synod, as might have been foreseen, lost little time in putting the New Lights out, via heresy proceedings. Next, they formed an independent Springfield Presbytery. But like all radicals, they found it easier to keep going than to apply the brakes. In 1804 the Springfield Presbytery fell apart. Stone and some of his friends joined with others in a new body,

On the Care and Feeding of Evangelists

Perhaps I may say a few things right here that may be of some little benefit to my brethren in the ministry. You know these are the days of sore throats and bronchial affections among preachers. . . .

Now, without professing to have studied physiology, or to be skilled in the science of medicine, I beg leave, with very humble pretensions, to give it as my opinion that most cases of these diseases are brought on by carelessness and inattention of public speakers themselves. I had, for several years previous to the great revival of 1843, been greatly afflicted with the bronchial affection; so much so that I really thought the days of my public ministry were well-nigh over. This revival lasted near five months, through a hard and cold winter. I preached, exhorted, sung, prayed, and labored at the altar, I need not say several times a day or night, but almost day and night for months together.

With many fears I entered on this work, but from the beginning I threw myself under restraint, took time to respire freely between sentences, commanded the modulation and cadence of my voice, avoided singing to fatigue, avoided sudden transitions from heat to cold, and when I left the atmosphere of the church, heated by the stoves and breath of the crowd, guarded my breast and throat, and even mouth, from a sudden and direct contact with the chilling air, or air of any kind; got to my room as quick as possible, slept in no cold rooms if I could help it; bathed my throat and breast every morning with fresh, cold water from the well or spring; wore no tight stocks or cravats; breathed freely; and, strange to tell, I came out of the five months' campaign of a revival much sounder than when I entered it.

The only medicine I used at all was a little cayenne pepper and table salt dissolved in cold vinegar, and this just as I was leaving a warm atmosphere to go into the cold air or wind; and although several years have passed since, I have been very little troubled with that disease, and can preach as long and as loud as is necessary for any minister . . .

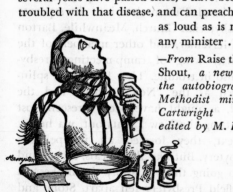

—From Raise the Heavenly Shout, *a new version of the autobiography of the Methodist minister Peter Cartwright (1785–1872), edited by M. F. K. Fisher.*

shorn of titles and formality, which carried the magnificently simple name of the Christian Church. Later on, Stone went over to the followers of Thomas and Alexander Campbell, who called themselves Disciples of Christ. Richard McNemar, after various spiritual adventures, became a Shaker. Thus, ten years after Cane Ridge, the score was depressing for Presbyterians. Revivalism had brought on innumerable arguments, split off whole presbyteries, and sent ministers and congregations flying into the arms of at least four other church groups. That splintering was a stronger indictment than any conservative could have invented to bring against Cane Ridge, or against its western child, the camp meeting.

A dead end appeared to have been reached. But it was only a second-act curtain. In the first act, religion in the West, given up for lost, had been saved by revivalism. In the second, grown strong and rambunctious, it had quarreled with its eastern parents. Now the time was at hand for a third-act resolution of the drama. Both sides would have to back down and compromise. For the lesson of history was already plain. In religious matters, as in all matters, East and West, metropolis and frontier, were not really warring opposites. Each nourished the other, and each had an impact on the other. Whatever emerged as "American" would carry some of the imprint of both, or it would perish.

On the part of the West, the retreat consisted of taming the camp meeting. Oddly enough, it was not the Presbyterians who did that. By 1812 or so, they had drawn back from it, afraid of its explosive qualities. But the Methodists were in an excellent position to make use of revivalism and all its trappings. They had, at that time at least, no educated conservative wing. They welcomed zealous backwood preachers, even if they were grammatically deficient. In fact, they worked such men into their organization and sent them, under the name of "circuit-riders," traveling tirelessly on horseback to every lonely settlement that the wilderness spawned. The result was that the Methodists were soon far in the lead in evangelizing the frontier. They did not have to worry about the claims of limited election either. Their formal theology did not recognize it. With a plain-spoken and far-reaching ministry freely offering salvation to all true believers, Methodism needed only some kind of official harvest season to count and bind together the converts. The camp meeting was the perfect answer. By 1811, the Methodists had held four or five hundred of them throughout the country; by 1820, they had held a thousand—by far the majority of all such gatherings in the nation.

But these meetings were not replicas of Cane Ridge.

They were combed, washed, and made respectable. Permanent sites were picked, regular dates chosen, and preachers and flocks given ample time to prepare. When meeting time came, the arriving worshipers in their wagons were efficiently taken in charge, told where to park their vehicles and pasture their teams, and given a spot for their tents. Orderly rows of these tents surrounded a preaching area equipped with sturdy benches and preaching stands. The effect was something like that of a formal bivouac just before a general's inspection. Tight scheduling kept the worship moving according to plan—dawn prayers, eight o'clock sermons, eleven o'clock sermons, dinner breaks, afternoon prayers and sermons, meals again, and candlelight services. Years of experience tightened the schedules, and camp-meeting manuals embodied the fruits of practice. Regular hymns replaced the discordant bawling of the primitive era. Things took on a generally homelike look. There were Methodist ladies who did not hesitate to bring their best feather beds to spread in the tents, and meals tended to be planned and ample affairs. Hams, turkeys, gravies, biscuits, preserves, and melons produced contented worshipers and happy memories.

There were new rules to cope with disorderliness as well. Candles, lamps, and torches fixed to trees kept the area well lit and discouraged young converts from amorous ways. Guards patrolled the circumference of the camp, and heroic if sometimes losing battles were fought to keep whiskey out. In such almost decorous surroundings jerks, barks, dances and trances became infrequent and finally nonexistent.

Not that there was a total lack of enthusiasm. Hymns were still yelled and stamped as much as sung. Nor was it out of bounds for the audience to pepper the sermon with ejaculations of "Amen!" and "Glory!" Outsiders were still shocked by some things they saw. But they did not realize how far improvement had gone.

Eastern churchmen had to back down somewhat, too. Gradually, tentatively, they picked up the revival and made it part of their religious life. In small eastern towns it became regularized into an annual season of "ingathering," like the harvest or the election. Yet it could not be contained within neat, white-painted meeting-houses. Under the "sivilized" clothing, the tattered form of Twain's Pap Finn persisted. Certain things were taken for granted after a time. The doctrine of election was bypassed and, in practice, allowed to wither away.

Moreover, a new kind of religious leader, the popular evangelist, took the stage. Men like Charles G. Finney in the 1830's, Dwight L. Moody in the 1870's, and Billy Sunday in the decade just preceding the First World War flashed into national prominence. Their meetings overflowed church buildings and spilled into convention halls, auditoriums, and specially built "tabernacles." As it happened, these men came from lay ranks into preaching. Finney was a lawyer, Moody a shoe salesman, and Sunday a baseball player. They spoke down-to-earth language to their massed listeners, reduced the Bible to basic axioms, and drew their parables from the courtroom, the market, and the barnyard. They made salvation the only goal of their service, and at the meeting's end they beckoned the penitents forward to acknowledge the receipt of grace. In short, they carried on the camp-meeting tradition. By the closing years of the nineteenth century, however, the old campgrounds for the most part were slowly abandoned. Growing cities swallowed them up, and rapid transportation destroyed the original reason for the prolonged camp-out. But the meetings were not dead. Mass revivalism had moved them indoors and made them a permanent part of American Protestantism.

All of this cost something in religious depth, religious learning, religious dignity. Yet there was not much choice. The American churches lacked the support of an all-powerful state or of age-old traditions. They had to move with the times. That is why their history is so checkered with schismatic movements—symptoms of the struggle to get in step with the parade. Hence, if the West in 1800 could not ignore religion, the rest of the country, in succeeding years, could not ignore the western notion of religion. One student of the camp meeting has said that it flourished "side by side with the militia muster, with the cabin raising and the political barbecue." That was true, and those institutions were already worked deeply into the American grain by 1840. They reflected a spirit of democracy, optimism, and impatience that would sweep us across a continent, sweep us into industrialism, sweep us into a civil war. That spirit demanded some religious expression, some promise of a millennium in which all could share.

The camp meeting was part of that religious expression, part of the whole revival system that channeled American impulses into churchgoing ways. In the home of the brave, piety was organized so that Satan got no breathing spells. Neither, for that matter, did anyone else.

Bernard A. Weisberger, associate professor of history at Wayne State University, has contributed to previous issues of AMERICAN HERITAGE. *This article is adapted from his recent book,* They Gathered at the River, *published by Little, Brown and Company.*

Roofs over Rivers

CONTINUED FROM PAGE 34

knocked them free himself, and since the previous day the bridge had been standing alone. The huge span was aptly named "The Colossus." It stood for 26 years before being destroyed by fire in 1838.

The Colossus made Lewis Wernwag's reputation, and for the next quarter century he was seldom without contracts to build covered bridges. Moving to Harpers Ferry, Virginia, in 1824, he took his designs into the fast-developing country west of the Alleghenies, and his sons built specially designed Wernwag arch bridges on the turnpikes of Ohio, Kentucky, and Indiana.

A third early builder was Theodore Burr of Torringford, Connecticut. A self-taught housebuilder and millwright, he put up several experimental bridges before finally concentrating on a simple arch, stiffened with timber bracing and supporting a level roadway. Burr's were the first bridges of any size to cross such rivers as the Hudson, the Mohawk, the Delaware, and the Susquehanna.

An easygoing optimist, Theodore Burr was not awed

WHEN KNIGHTHOOD WAS IN FLOWER

BY PERMISSION OF THE NEW YORK Herald Tribune

by having four big bridges across the Susquehanna all under construction at once. He even bid on a fifth, at Columbia-Wrightsville, Pennsylvania. Burr's proposal for a 5,620-foot span—more than a mile of wooden trusses—was made on a piece of scrap paper. He promised to construct the piers and abutments for $66,000 and the frame, "or superstructure," for $54,000, to secure the bridge from the weather for $8,900, and to floor it for another $8,500. At the bottom he added: "Superintendence, say $6,450."

Burr's bid was a bit high, and the job went to another Connecticut builder, Jonathan Walcott. Thus Burr lost out on the distinction of erecting what was to be the longest multiple-span covered wooden bridge ever built in the world. He had to be satisfied with building the longest with a single span.

This was at McCall's Ferry, Pennsylvania, a narrow constriction in the Susquehanna where the water ran 150 feet deep. Since scaffolding could not be driven this deep, the resourceful Burr pinned the span together on land and started to move it into position on floats. When, in the dead of winter, the river froze tight, he finished the job by skidding the arch into place on the ice. To secure manpower, he played up sectional rivalry between the counties on either side of the river, and induced the farmers who would ultimately pay for using the bridge to help him erect it. When McCall's Ferry Bridge was finished, it had a clear span of over 360 feet. Even today's laminated wooden arches, prefabricated and lifted aloft by derricks in the construction of huge airplane hangars and public arenas, have not yet equaled the length of Burr's mighty arch of 1815.

Despite all the work that went into it, this record-holding bridge stood for only three years; it was destroyed in an ice jam and never replaced. But although the inventor died in 1822, his arch bridges lived on. His boss-carpenters became contractors themselves and bridged countless lesser streams in New York, Pennsylvania, Ohio, and Indiana. Their sons and apprentices took the tried-and-true Burr arch even farther afield, using it for railroad spans in New England and highway bridges from Nova Scotia to California.

The big timbers that went into the elaborate structures of Palmer, Wernwag, and Burr took considerable manpower to put together. There was a crying need for a simple bridge that could be erected by a common carpenter's gang. Ithiel Town, an architect from New Haven, Connecticut, filled the bill in 1820 with the patenting of his "Town lattice truss" bridge, an all-wood arrangement of planks crisscrossed like a garden fence and pinned together with big two-inch wooden pegs. Weight placed on it only tightened its framework.

Town promoted the bridge throughout the eastern states while carrying out his main work of designing churches and public buildings. The lattice truss caught on slowly, but eventually it became the favorite type of construction in New England. Town received a royalty of one dollar per foot for patent rights, and two dollars a foot if one of his sharp-eyed agents discovered a bridge erected on the plan without prior permission. New England emigrants took the Town lattice truss with them to Ohio and Michigan, and there was even one built (without a roof) over the Jordan River in Salt Lake City.

In these early years, bridge engineering was a matter of trial and error. In 1829, Colonel Stephen H. Long of the U.S. Army Topographical Engineers devised the first scientific wooden-truss bridge in America. It was essentially a series of crossed beams pinned into square frames. The Colonel called it the Jackson Bridge, in honor of the President, and built the first one as a highway overpass over the B&O Railroad outside Baltimore. It was the first railway grade-crossing separation in America.

Since Colonel Long, famed for his western explorations, was primarily a railway engineer, many of his bridges were built on the new rail lines of the 1830's. The first railroad drawbridges—over the Passaic and Hackensack rivers in New Jersey—followed his plans, as did the first combined railroad and highway bridge, over the Raritan River at New Brunswick, New Jersey. It is recounted that, when caught in the inky interior of the New Brunswick bridge while a train rumbled across the roof, more than one horse died of sheer fright!

Long's bridges enjoyed a popularity of ten years, during which they vied with Ithiel Town's lattice trusses for use by the growing rail network. The rival promoters exchanged polite notes via the newspapers, waxing eloquent in praise of their respective designs. Colonel Long, busy with army matters, finally left his share of the battle to his brother and "General Agent," Dr. Moses Long of Warner, New Hampshire. Dr. Long, who was also the town postmaster, used his free franking privilege to blanket the East with advertising broadsides extolling the virtues of the "Long patent bridge." Ithiel Town countered by appearing in person at bridge contract-lettings to plead the merits of his "mode," sometimes—if the bridge were to be large or to stand in a prominent location—offering to waive his royalties.

After 1840, both the Town and the Long patent bridges were almost totally eclipsed by another design, using wooden cross-frames and iron rods and invented by William Howe of Spencer, Massachusetts. Howe

WHOA, YOU FOOLS! WHOA!

J.R.WILLIAMS 3-27

BORN THIRTY YEARS TOO SOON

came from a family of inventors: his brother Tyler devised a spring bed, and his nephew Elias achieved lasting fame for his sewing machine.

The Howe truss had a lot of the features of Long's bridge, and the Colonel cried "infringement" long and loud, but to no avail. The basic difference was in the introduction of the iron rods and turnbuckles with which the Howe bridge could easily be trued up by tightening a few nuts. This ease of erection and maintenance made the Howe truss a special favorite of the railroads, and enabled them to span a stream quickly during the period when they were hastily laying new track in all directions. All the pieces for a wooden Howe truss bridge could be pre-cut and loaded on a brace of flat cars. Add the iron rods, plus a crew of husky Irish laborers, and the cars could be pushed out to a pair of waiting abutments at the end of the track. Twenty-four hours would usually see a 100-foot bridge in place; it could be roofed and sided while it was in service.

With the advent of William Howe, bridgebuilding became big business. Gone were the primitive posters and word-of-mouth advertising. Howe had four brothers-in-law named Stone who set up a family dynasty of bridgebuilding firms with the rights to build Howe truss bridges in specified localities. Amasa Stone had Ohio; brother Joseph, New England; brother Daniel, Pennsylvania and New Jersey. Andros Stone took *his* brother-in-law into partnership to work westward out of Chicago. In a few short years, Howe truss bridges were practically standard on railroads, and still more companies were formed to build them. (Some seventeen of these spans still stand in the Northwest.) There was enough work out of St. Louis to induce the firm of Stone and Boomer to buy an entire wooded township in Missouri, where they built a model mill town to work the trees into bridge timbers.

With the big towns, the turnpikes, and the railroads provided for, local carpenters turned their attention to the smaller villages and secondary roads. Not wishing to pay royalties, these home-town artisans designed their own bridges. They used, for the most part, simple trusses on the same principles of roof framing and support that had gone into many thousands of houses and barns.

There were odd, one-of-a-kind bridges, of course. In 1841, two Maryland men collaborated in patenting a "puzzle-keyed" bridge. Though never actually built,

BORN THIRTY YEARS TOO SOON

their whole structure was designed to hang on a single piece, which if removed would send the entire fabrication tumbling into the river!

A Pennsylvania schoolmaster named Herman Haupt, in charge of a girls' seminary in Gettysburg, experimented incessantly with little bridge models, loading them to the breaking point with dangling lead weights. In 1839 he finally devised and patented one that satisfied him, but due to the inception of the Howe truss shortly afterward, Haupt's bridge was never popular, and his fame rests more on his work as a Civil War general in charge of military railroads.

The heyday of covered bridges was about 1860. They were common both in country and city, on turnpike and byway. Major eastern centers, such as Hartford, Springfield, Philadelphia, Baltimore, Washington, Richmond, Columbia, and Augusta, as well as Pitts-

burgh, Cleveland, Columbus, Dayton, and Indianapolis to the west, all had covered bridges. Later years even saw one erected in Los Angeles. Records show that they once stood in all but eleven states.

After the Civil War came the age of iron. The covered bridges—sometimes perfectly sound ones that were simply thought to be old-fashioned—were gradually replaced. Oddly enough, iron-smelting Pennsylvania bucked the trend. Their own wrought-iron and steel channels and beams were all right for building bridges elsewhere, but at home the Keystone Staters kept right on building them of wood. There are more than 1,300 covered bridges still standing in the nation today, and Pennsylvania leads the other states, with 351 as of September, 1958. Ohio had approximately 240 by unofficial count in the same year. In Indiana, where covered bridges were built from 1880 right down to World War I—some of them with fancy embellishments, scrolls, and gingerbread decorations—over 150 covered bridges still stand. Oregon is next with 130-odd, and then comes Vermont with 106. New Hampshire, Alabama, West Virginia, and Georgia still have a good representation, and there are 29 covered railroad bridges in New England and the Far West. In most of the other states, however, the day of the covered bridge has passed, and only a few isolated examples remain.

Yet even today, in areas where steel shipments are costly and wood is plentiful, covered bridges are still being built. In Lane County, Oregon, for example, a few modern ones are planned and built by engineers every year, particularly in newly developed areas where the need for heavier bridges has not yet been established.

Recently, residents of the Massachusetts towns of Charlemont and Sheffield petitioned the Commonwealth's Department of Public Works to replace their old bridges in kind. The contractors looked over the elaborate plans for modern three-lane covered bridges, and then realized that there were no timbers in all New England big enough to meet the specifications. So both Charlemont and Sheffield have shiny new covered bridges, built in 1951 and 1953, respectively, but the wood that went into their construction came all the way from Oregon!

Richard Sanders Allen, postmaster of Round Lake, New York (population, 1,000), is an engineering historian. His specialty is covered bridges, but he has written on everything from colonial roads to pioneer aviation. His Covered Bridges of the Northeast *was published in 1957; a companion volume,* Covered Bridges of the Middle Atlantic States, *is due out this fall.*

The Last of the Bosses

CONTINUED FROM PAGE 25

city, the massed wards south of the Back Bay—these were his roots, and he never really functioned outside them. Before his second term was up, he resigned to enter the 1913 mayoralty contest.

Fitzgerald's first thought that year was to run again for mayor, but young Jim Curley—back from Washington, aggressive and dominating—was like a tidal wave. Honey Fitz's second thought was to retire. The ward bosses finally fixed on an opponent, a Fitzgerald nonentity named Thomas J. Kenny.

Curley's campaign for mayor dwarfed his congressional one of four years before. He stormed the autumn city in raccoon coat, "iron mike" on his head and the gilded voice booming. He promised to clean out City Hall and give it back to the people—whatever that might mean. He savaged the ward bosses and invited the voters to call on him personally at City Hall. He promised more schools and playgrounds and beaches and parks and jobs. Politicians can hear the grass grow, and there was the underground feeling that he was unbeatable.

Incongruous as it might seem in later years, or even months, Curley was first hailed as a reform mayor. Hundreds of Honey Fitz's officeholders were ousted. True to his promise, Curley opened up City Hall. Those who wanted to see him about jobs, favors, or assistance, he received without appointment. A squad of secretaries catalogued each visitor before he was taken to the Mayor. Decisions were made on the spot. If a request could not be granted, Curley said so and why. He was the super-boss. Ward bosses became obsolete: Curley had destroyed their power, even in Ward 17. He talked to an average of 200 persons a day, 50,000 in a year.

The financial and business community's satisfaction with the new mayor was brutally short-lived. Curley, they would soon discover, had lost none of his old resentments. Assessments were raised all round. A vast construction program such as Boston had never seen before was begun. Streets were ripped up, transit lines extended, beaches and playgrounds laid out, hospitals built, and services expanded. There was a job for every jobless man in the city. Here lay Curley's basic formula, then and in all his administrations: a juggler's act of public works without regard for cost. When the city treasury was empty he would borrow. The outraged Yankees could pay for it all through taxes.

Yet, much of what he did needed to be done. The cost would be excessive, the payrolls padded, a percentage of the contractors' fees would always find its way into Curley's pocket—yet without him most of these projects would never have been undertaken. By the end of his first term he had altered the face of the city; by the end of his fourth term the tax rate had quintupled.

Though with him money went as easily as it came, though he liked to be known as the mayor of the poor, he enjoyed lush living. Midway in his first term he built himself the house overlooking Jamaica Pond that would be known as the House with the Shamrock Shutters. It was better than anything on Beacon Street. Some of the trimmings, including the mahogany-paneled dining room and the winding staircase, came from the Fairhaven house of Henry H. Rogers, the Standard Oil executive. The Finance Commission and others were to ask vainly how anyone could build a $60,000 house on a $15,000 lot on a salary of $10,000 a year. Such questions never bothered Curley. In his autobiography he maintained—archly and without expecting to be believed—that he had made the money for his house on a stock market tip given him by a since-deceased wool merchant. Almost everyone in Boston knew that the house had been a donation from a contractor. The Curley wards felt he deserved it.

In 1917, when Curley ran for re-election, a curious amalgam of businessmen and bosses took the field against him. Martin Lomasney, the old Ward 8 mahatma and the only ward boss to survive unscathed, entered two congressmen with Celtic names as pseudo-candidates to cut into Curley's Irish-Democratic vote. It was an old gambit, used many times by Curley himself, and it worked well enough to defeat Curley.

After several ludicrously unfortunate business ventures—in such matters Curley would always be both gullible and inept—he became president of the Hibernia National Bank, within wistful sight of City Hall. But this was for him only an interlude. His real life was always politics.

The 1921 mayoralty campaign was one of the closest and meanest in the history of Boston, and Curley fought alone. No political pro in the city was for him, and the betting against him ran over two to one. But his opponent, a respected Catholic lawyer named John R. Murphy, was not prepared for what he now had to face —too much of a gentleman, it was said commiseratingly of him afterward. Among other things, Curley sent some of his workers to Charlestown dressed in clerical black and carrying prayer books. There they let it be known that turncoat Murphy had joined the Masons and that he was divorcing his wife to marry a sixteen-year-old girl. Other Curley supporters rang doorbells through Catholic South Boston posing as members of the Hawes Baptist Club and soliciting votes for John

R. Murphy. Curley even gave a Ku Klux Klan organizer known as the Black Pope $2,000 to campaign against him.

Against all odds and predictions Curley won, with 74,200 votes to Murphy's 71,800. For the first time in a Boston election women could vote, and it was generally felt that Mary Curley's "Personal Appeal to Women Voters," an open letter circulated at the last minute, gave her husband the extra votes that elected him.

Before anyone quite knew what was happening—anyone except Curley—there were $24,000,000 worth of building projects under way. Several times the city treasury gave out, and Curley merely borrowed more money against future taxes. If a banker showed reluctance to lend, Curley would threaten to start a run on his bank "a mile long." Taxes and assessments as well as buildings went up.

During Curley's second administration, and with Curley pointedly in mind, the Republican state legislature passed a law that no mayor of Boston might succeed himself. Instead, in 1924 Curley ran as Democratic candidate for governor against Alvan T. Fuller, who would later become so widely known in connection with the Sacco-Vanzetti case. It was a Republican year, and in any case, Massachusetts would not be ready for Curley until after the transvaluations of the depression. Curley tried to make an issue of the Ku Klux Klan and his own opposition to it. Wherever he spoke in the rural sections of the state, fiery crosses would suddenly blaze out on nearby hills just in time for him to point to them and say, voice resonant with emotion: "There it burns, the cross of hatred upon which Our Lord, Jesus Christ, was crucified." Later he admitted that the crosses had been touched off by his boys. Fuller won—but the size of Curley's vote gave the state party leaders, whose enthusiasm for Curley was at best limited, something to think about.

In the presidential election of 1928 the Commonwealth of Massachusetts was one of the eight states carried by Al Smith. To the Irish Democrats of the Commonwealth, Smith was the most creditable man from Irish ranks who had yet appeared in politics. Before the national convention the Massachusetts leaders were solidly for Smith. All of them were at odds with Curley, and they took care that the ex-mayor would have no part in the convention or in the subsequent Smith campaign. They reckoned, however, without Curley.

Shortly after Smith's nomination, Curley opened what he called his Bull Pen in the vacant Young's Hotel near City Hall. He had the walls plastered with Smith signs and photographs. There were loudspeakers in the windows blaring a steady raucous mixture of speeches and music. Every day was open house in the Bull Pen. Inside it was like an amateur night. Anyone who felt like walking in and speaking his piece about Smith was welcome to use the microphone. And when Al Smith arrived in Boston to ride through the city in a whirl of ticker tape, the excluded Curley was somehow there in the car beside him, to the chagrin of the official members of the party. Yet in the election, when Smith was trailing Hoover by 83,000 votes outside Boston, and the city's roaring majority gave him the state by 17,000, it was Curley's desperate drumming up of the last few thousand votes that made the difference.

After the Hoover sweep Curley was astute enough to realize that Smith would not have another chance, no matter what Massachusetts Democrats thought. Four years later Curley was the first and in fact the only politician in the state to come out for Franklin Roosevelt before the convention. Massachusetts Democrats, still solidly and emotionally for Smith, were shocked and furious. Curley was a traitor. The wilderness was where he belonged.

The Massachusetts delegation to the 1932 Democratic Convention was headed by Governor Joseph B. Ely, an old Curley enemy. Curley would not be a delegate to this convention; in fact if Ely had anything to say about it he would not even be a spectator. But, as the event again showed, one had better not count Curley out too soon. For directly behind the Massachusetts delegation in the convention hall sat the Puerto Ricans with their chairman—none other than Alcalde Jaime Miguel Curleo. The Alcalde, in a familiarly florid accent, cast the six Puerto Rican votes for Roosevelt, though even after the Roosevelt stampede the Massachusetts delegation glumly and stubbornly held out to the end for Smith. Behind the scenes, Curley had helped arrange with Hearst and Garner the deal that finally gave Roosevelt the nomination.

Public opinion in Massachusetts veered quickly. The emotions that for four years had been bound up with the fortunes of Al Smith were transferred overnight to Roosevelt. Having left Boston as an outcast, Curley came back from Chicago a hero. He arrived in North Station to find that a crowd of 250,000 had turned out to meet him. Streets were jammed all the way to the Common. Inside the station 21 bands were blaring at one another. It took 100 reserve policemen to clear a path for Curley to his car.

From that night until the election all Curley's efforts went into the campaign. He reopened his "Bull Pen," and re-decorated it with large Roosevelt motifs. He mortgaged the House with the Shamrock Shutters. He traveled 10,000 miles through 23 western and midwestern states to deliver 140 speeches. For the election he spent a quarter of a million dollars of his own money. With James Roosevelt as an assistant, he was the Roosevelt ringmaster in Massachusetts.

All this activity had not been undertaken just for the Forgotten Man. What Curley now wanted was to set the seal of respectability on his career by becoming the next Secretary of the Navy. After all, it was a job held recently by a Boston Adams. Shortly after the election Curley, with his daughter Mary, called on Roosevelt at Warm Springs. There, according to Curley, Roosevelt told him, "Well, Jim, if that's what you want, the job is yours." A few weeks later, however, at Calvin Coolidge's funeral in Northampton, James Roosevelt took Curley aside and told him a Cabinet post wasn't possible. James went on to tell him that he might instead become ambassador to France or Italy, and suggested that he drop in at the White House to talk it over.

On that visit the President mentioned Italy, and Curley asked for a few days to think it over. Whether Roosevelt ever intended to send the boss of Boston to Rome, whether Boston's William Cardinal O'Connell vetoed the idea, or whether Curley was being given the Roosevelt run-around—no one will ever know. In any event, at Curley's next interview, the smiling President said there were difficulties about Italy and offered him instead the post of ambassador to Poland, remarking that Poland was one of the most interesting places in the world. "If it is such a goddam interesting place," Curley is said to have replied, "why don't you resign the Presidency and take it yourself?" To the newsmen who crowded around him outside, he used a quick term to describe Roosevelt that Truman later reserved for music critics. In Boston a witticism went the rounds that if he had accepted, he would have paved the Polish Corridor.

Between the two conventions Curley had been elected mayor for the third time, by a clear majority and once more with the odds against him. His principal opponent was another respectable Democratic lawyer, Frederick W. Mansfield, silently endorsed by Cardinal O'Connell himself, who had long felt with increasing irritation that Curley was a discredit both to the Irish and his Church. The Cardinal, from a slum background similar to Curley's, was of the cast of a Renaissance prelate. He spoke Italian like an Italian, English like a cultivated Englishman. An urbane and aristocratic man, he wanted to see the emergent Irish become respectable and accepted. Politically, however, the Cardinal was an innocent.

Curley in his inaugural address attacked the Republican Good Government Association and the "select and exclusive body of social bounders in the Back Bay." His new administration began with the usual Curley public works projects, the need for which was accentuated now by the onset of the depression.

Even before his election he knew that his wife was doomed by cancer. She died the following June. Mary Curley's influence on her husband had been stabilizing and restraining. Without her he seemed to lose his balance. He drank too much, he coarsened physically, he grew bombastic and careless, he had less control over his quick temper. Opposing Ely's nomination for governor, he got into a fist fight with the chairman of the Democratic State Committee at radio station WNAC. City Hall interested him less now than national politics.

The older, less careful Curley now made a political mistake. He made his friend Edmund L. Dolan city treasurer. Dolan was the legal owner of Curley's 93-foot yacht, punningly named *Maicaway*. As Curley's understudy, Dolan headed the Mohawk Packing Company and the Legal Securities Corporation. Mohawk was organized to provide meat for city institutions—at a third above the usual cost. Through the Legal Securities Corporation, Dolan managed to sell bonds to the city and also buy them from the city to sell to brokers, collecting commissions at both ends. The state-appointed Finance Commission uncovered these and certain aspects of land-takings and other facts sufficient, so it seemed for a while, to send both Curley and Dolan to jail. The younger Curley would never have left himself so vulnerable.

Eventually Dolan was charged with the theft of more than $170,000 from the city. Before the case came to trial he was caught trying to bribe the jury, and received two and a half years in jail. At the same time a bill in equity was brought against Curley, and after three years and 34 continuances he was ordered to pay back $42,629 to the city treasury.

Now that he had no more Washington ambitions he badgered and needled Roosevelt for more aid, more money for Boston. He devised new projects for the Civil Works Administration. After all, a CWA was what he had been occupied with all his political life. With Governor Ely, still a disgruntled Smith man, retiring in 1934, Curley had little trouble in getting the Democratic nomination for governor. That election, the second New Deal wave, swept almost the complete Democratic state ticket into office. Boston had taken over Massachusetts at last. The crowd from City Hall moved up Beacon Hill to the State House.

Curley's two-year term as governor marked both the height and depths of his career. No such turmoil had occurred on Beacon Hill since cynical, droop-eyed Ben Butler had been governor fifty years before. Curley would now use the greater resources of the Commonwealth as he had previously used those of the city, but this time with a recklessness and a hard arrogance he had not shown before. Work there was, projects useful and otherwise, feverishly undertaken from the Berkshires to Cape Cod, and where there was no work there were at least jobs. The State House offices bulged with idle incompetents, the Governor's anterooms swarmed with old City Hall petitioners. When the Finance Commission still threatened to dig up old Curley City Hall scandals, its members were bribed or dismissed. Curley rode roughshod over the Governor's Council, courts, and department heads, his energy as boundless as his activities were unregulated.

Insolence of office trailed him through the state as he scorched the roads in his limousine with its S–1 license plates, preceded by state police motorcycle escorts with sirens wailing, and followed by carloads of his military aides bright in incongruous blue and gold-braid uniforms. S–1 was in a series of accidents. One state trooper was killed, another badly injured. Curley moved across the Massachusetts landscape like a Latin dictator. For the 1936 Harvard Tercentenary he arrived at the Yard escorted by scarlet-coated National Lancers, drums beating and trumpets sounding, to move ostentatiously past a stony-faced President Roosevelt while a few Harvard die-hards booed.

Just before he took the oath of office, Curley had swung a parting punch at Governor Ely. Somehow that outrageous brawl within the State House became symbolic of his administration. The inauguration ball, held at the Armory, was a monstrous affair to which 14,000 were invited. During his first year in office the Governor spent $85,206 just for taxis, flowers, dinners, luncheons, cigars, refreshments, and trips for himself and his guests and secretaries. The following winter he moved his entire staff to Florida. In those depression times his daughter Mary's wedding to Edward C. Donnelly, Jr., of the Donnelly Advertising Company, was the gaudiest ever held in Massachusetts. The bride's trousseau cost $10,000—paid for, and not donated, as anti-Curleyites had hinted. At the packed Cathedral of the Holy Cross, under the dismayed eyes of Cardinal O'Connell, many of those present stood on the pews as the bride and her father came down the aisle. There were 2,300 guests at the Copley Plaza reception afterward. They downed two tons of lobster at $13 a plate.

Financially buttressed at the end of his governor's term, Curley determined to revenge himself on Roosevelt. The President had not liked him as governor, and he would like still less to find him in the United States Senate. For Governor Curley the senatorial nomination was easy to manipulate; the election seemed equally so. His Republican opponent was Henry Cabot

Lodge, Jr., the grandson of the old anti-League senator, whose political experience was contained in two terms in the Massachusetts legislature. Curley liked to refer to him as "Little Boy Blue." Yet in the New Deal landslide of 1936, when every other major Democratic candidate in the Commonwealth was overwhelmingly elected, Curley lost to Lodge by 136,000 votes. All the states except Maine and Vermont went for Roosevelt, but Massachusetts had had enough of James Michael Curley.

In a sense, however, Curley had the last word, for on that day when the cannon boomed across the Common to announce a new governor, he stole the whole show by marrying again. His second wife, Gertrude Casey Dennis, was a widow, a quiet woman without political or social ambitions, who would give him the domestic stability he had found in his first wife.

The following year he again ran for mayor, and again found himself opposed by a "reform" candidate,

CURLEY THE THUG

On October 4, 1926, the day before this cartoon appeared in the Boston Telegraph, Curley knocked down Publisher F. W. Enwright on the street. On October 5 and 6 Enwright struck back with two cartoons—this one referring to a jail sentence Curley had served in 1904—and an editorial. Curley sued for libel; Enwright was imprisoned, and his paper folded. Mysteriously, these two issues are missing from Telegraph files in the Boston Public Library.

Maurice Tobin, a handsome and hardy young Democrat from his own district, who in the wheel-spins of politics would twice become mayor, then governor, and finally figurehead Secretary of Labor in Truman's Cabinet. Curley has accurately described him as "a protégé of mine who learned too fast." It was to Curley's mind an easy election, but on election morning there appeared on the masthead of the Boston *Post,* whose editorials generally reflected the views of the archdiocese, a brief notice to the voters of Boston that read: "Cardinal O'Connell, in speaking to the Catholic Alumni Association, said, 'The walls are raised against honest men in civic life.' You can break down these walls by voting for an honest, clean, competent young man, Maurice Tobin, today. . . ."

Thousands of copies of the *Post* were distributed free in front of all the churches. The actual quotation was from an address made by the Cardinal six years before, but few readers noticed that the quotation ended before Tobin was mentioned. To the faithful it seemed that His Eminence had endorsed Curley's opponent. Curley furiously tried to get a retraction broadcast, but the Cardinal could not be reached. It was a maneuver worthy of Curley himself. Enough pious votes were swung to Tobin for him to win.

In 1938 Curley was strong enough to take the nomination away from the Democratic governor, but he was still unable to win the election. His opponent was the long-jawed speaker of the Massachusetts House of Representatives, Leverett Saltonstall, who as a Republican, a Harvard man, and a Brahmin combined the three things that Curley was best at excoriating. Yet Saltonstall was a new type of Old Yankee who represented a *rapprochement* with what Curley liked to call "the newer races." The growing numbers of middle-class Irish liked him. In later years when he and young Senator Kennedy were colleagues in Washington, they became so friendly that Kennedy refused to endorse Saltonstall's next Democratic opponent. Saltonstall also had the advantage of owning one of the most agreeably ugly mugs in politics. Curley made the mistake of quipping that Saltonstall might have a South Boston face but he would never dare show it in South Boston. Of course, Saltonstall walked through the South Boston streets the next day, talking with everyone he met and dropping in at the innumerable bars. He overwhelmed Curley at the polls.

By the time of Boston's next municipal election Mayor Tobin had built a tight political machine of his own. Curley ran against him nevertheless and suffered his fourth defeat in a row. At 67, after a generation in politics, it looked as if he had come to the end of the road. But that was not the way Curley saw it.

He turned again to his solid core of supporters in the close wards of Roxbury and South Boston and Charlestown. As if he were now going down the ladder he had once climbed, he turned to them to send him back to Congress in 1942.

These days he was short of funds, and every week there was the $500 installment on the $42,629 he had been ordered to pay the city. A few months before Pearl Harbor, unlucky as usual in his private ventures, he had run into a Washington promoter named James G. Fuller, who was organizing a five-percenter corporation to mediate between manufacturers looking for war contracts and the appropriate heads of government agencies. Fuller offered to make Curley president of this organization, to be known as the Engineers' Group, Inc. Later, Fuller was shown to be a confidence man and ex-convict. Curley, in spite of his title, had little to do with Fuller's group except to appear on the letterhead, and before he became a congressman he had resigned.

Two years later, however, the Engineers' Group was one of those investigated by the Truman Committee, and sometime afterward Curley was indicted because of his connection with it. He always maintained that the case against him was directed from the White House. His trial was postponed, however, to allow him to run for mayor of Boston in November, 1945.

Tobin had moved on to become governor. The acting mayor was an obscurity, as were the other four candidates. Postwar Boston itself seemed derelict, a fading seaport as drab as the blackout paint that covered the gilt dome of the State House. So much needed doing, from street repairs to veterans' housing, and "Curley gets things done." That at least was the campaign slogan spread casually in public by his paid workers and taken up by others. Looking back to the prewar days, it seemed true enough. What if Curley was under indictment for some contract swindle? If he was guilty he hadn't done very much, no more than the rest of them. Anyhow, he got things done!

On election day Curley beat his closest opponent by two to one. For the fourth time he became mayor of Boston, 31 years after his first inaugural. Two months later he was convicted by a Washington jury of using the mails to defraud.

His final appeal to the Supreme Court was rejected in 1947. As the date neared for his sentencing he took to his bed. He received the last rites, and then unexpectedly his health picked up. Finally, the postponed but inevitable day came when he appeared in court, in a wheel chair and wearing a collar a size too large. His lawyer produced a certified list of nine ailments from which he was suffering, any one of which might prove fatal. Unimpressed, the judge sentenced him to six to eighteen months at the Federal Correctional Institute at Danbury, Connecticut. "You are sentencing me to die," Curley told him as they wheeled him away. Democratic House Leader John W. McCormack circulated a petition for Curley's release signed by all the Massachusetts delegation in Washington except Senator Kennedy. Finally after five months President Truman pardoned Curley—because, the President said later, "he was innocent."

Although it was not known at the time, or even later, Curley was shattered by his Danbury experience. There was nothing left of the young man who could shrug off a few months behind bars by reading all the books in the prison library. He now felt his age and a sense of failure, and for the first time he knew self-doubt. On his release, according to his daughter, he was hesitant about facing people again.

It warmed him to be met by a great milling crowd in front of the House with the Shamrock Shutters welcoming him with "Hail to the Chief." Inside he found familiar faces and a huge cake inscribed "Happy Birthday to Our Beloved Boss." In a few days he was back at City Hall at his old desk, looking fifteen years younger and running the city in his old way.

Yet the city was not the same. What he had done as boss of old Ward 17, and in his many years as mayor, had now become a more impersonal function of government. Voters were no longer gratefully held in line by a job shoveling snow, by the odd ton of coal, by the perennial Thanksgiving turkey and Christmas basket. Social security and unemployment insurance and the psychiatric social worker had taken over. The Irish were becoming middle class. One couldn't even soak the rich any more. In an almost bankrupt city the tax rate could go no higher. What Boston mostly needed now was an efficient receiver.

In the 1949 election Curley, to his derisive surprise, was opposed by John B. Hynes, who had served as mayor while Curley was in jail. "A little city clerk," Curley called him contemptuously, but when the ballots were counted, Hynes, the honest, skillful administrator, had won by 15,000 votes. It was the end of Curley's political career.

The next year by a twist of fate his daughter Mary and his son Leo both died of cerebral hemorrhages on the same day. Mary, who had been closest to him, had led an unhappy life; her marriage had ended in divorce in 1943. Leo was at his death a lieutenant in the Navy. In the father's loss even his enemies could feel a kindly pity for him.

After Curley got out of Danbury, he had complained to a Boston newspaperman named Joseph Dinneen that the press had always been unfair to him.

Dinneen then offered to write Curley's life story honestly and objectively as Curley told it to him. Curley agreed, and with his collaboration *The Purple Shamrock* was written. It appeared in 1949. Curley was proud of the book at the time and used to give away autographed copies to City Hall visitors.

The Purple Shamrock was the beginning of the Curley legend, the first attempt to put his career in perspective. What it told was true and often amazingly frank. Dinneen admitted that money was never a problem for Curley although he could never quite explain where he got it, that his income skyrocketed when he was in office and shrank to a trickle when he was not, that "there wasn't a contract awarded that did not have a cut for Curley." Yet Dinneen felt that even so, Curley's accomplishments justified the cuts.

Now that Curley was no longer to be feared politically he began to seem a kind of institution. He had been around for so long. Even the Bostonians who had fought him most in the pugnacious City Hall days, now in the nostalgia for their greener years felt a certain left-handed affection for him. He in turn was pleased and flattered by the occasional courtesy from a Lowell or a Lodge. Every political figure from Senator Saltonstall to the last South Boston ward heeler would drop in on the way past the House with the Shamrock Shutters. Curley in his old age could still charm the birds out of the trees.

When Edwin O'Connor's novel *The Last Hurrah* was scheduled to appear in 1956, it was carefully let out in advance that here was a novel about James Michael Curley. The editor of the *Globe* sent Curley a copy with the suggestion that he review it. The next day the book was returned with a note from Curley to the effect that he was consulting his lawyers.

Frank Skeffington, the politician-hero of the book, is undoubtedly Curley, even to his feud with the Cardinal, but he is a retouched Curley, less violent, more urbane. After Curley's first resentment had worn off, he began to see the Skeffington portrait as an asset. The book had toned down his ruthlessness, emphasized his benevolence. Various hints of fraud and peculation were, after all, no more than the admissions of *The Purple Shamrock*. For a while Curley took jokingly to calling and signing himself Skeffington. From originally intending to sue O'Connor, he ended up by congratulating him. *The Last Hurrah* caused him quite a lot of mental turmoil, however. As an aftermath he decided to write his autobiography, to out-Skeffington Skeffington by putting in what Dinneen had either not known or discreetly omitted.

In the final section of *The Last Hurrah*, when Skeffington is on his death bed, someone standing by the apparently unconscious figure remarks unctuously that if Skeffington had it all to do over again, he'd no doubt do it very differently. The dying man then manages to rouse himself and whisper: "The hell I would!" It is from this episode that Curley took the title of his own book, *I'd Do It Again*.

It is a rambling and uneven book, often dulled by the memory of obscure and forgotten ward heelers, but on the other hand enlivened by the candidly brazen quality of Curley's admissions. Though written by a professional rewrite man after conversations with Curley, it preserves Curley's own style of the informal cliché. What runs through the pages as an undercurrent, sensed even when not visible, is the after-feeling of the famine years, the old Celtic bitterness against the chill Yankee. Dinneen in reviewing it wrote that Curley had destroyed an illusion. *I'd Do It Again* is more reticent about Curley's financial background than is *The Purple Shamrock*. There is no mention of his income tax irregularities, and nothing is said of his connection—inadvertent though it may have been—with the Mishawum Manor blackmail scandal of the early twenties in which two district attorney friends of his were disbarred.

The summer after *The Last Hurrah* was published, Curley sold his Jamaicaway house to the Oblate Fathers. Those shamrock shutters, once a gesture of defiance, had become a familiar landmark. The furnishings, the library, the Georgian silver, the Waterford glass and Crown Derby china, jade and ivory *bibelots*, icons, pious statuary, and massive furniture had been purchased for the most part from auction rooms. Now to auction rooms they would return.

Curley moved to a small suburban-colonial house the other side of Jamaica Pond. He settled down there with his governor's chair and his mayor's chair and whatever other belongings were sizable enough to bring with him. Governor Foster Furcolo appointed him to a sinecure job, for Curley was hard up again. The Boston papers always seemed to be printing little human interest stories about him, photos of him fishing, or being shaved by Sal, the Huntington Avenue barber. Edward R. Murrow ran his Person-to-Person television show from the new house, and when Curley appeared he announced that he was going to live to be 125 years old so that he could bury all his enemies. Columbia Pictures was shooting a film version of *The Last Hurrah* starring Spencer Tracy.

Though Curley belittled it, from the time he moved his health began to fail. He was in and out of the hospital for check-ups. His face grew gray and flabby. Yet his right hand had not forgotten its cunning. When Columbia was preparing the *première* of *The Last Hurrah* Curley, after a private showing, filed suit for "irreparable damage to a valuable property"—that is, his life story. Columbia paid $25,000 for the damages. Then it was discovered that the lawyer to whom the check was made out was non-existent and that the stamp on the release was from a non-existent notary; it was claimed that the Curley signature was a forgery. Officially, no one knows yet who got the money. Curley still threatened suit, and Columbia settled for an additional $15,000. The picture was running at a Boston theater when he died.

He entered the city hospital for an intestinal operation on November 4, 1958, election day. Just another campaign, he remarked. For the first few days he seemed to be mending. He was able to walk about and to talk of the great Democratic victory. A week later he had a relapse. The end came quickly.

He lay on a bier in the State House in the great hall where the battle flags of Massachusetts regiments are kept, and in two days 100,000 people filed past. Then, on a warm morning like an aftermath of September, he was buried from Holy Cross Cathedral. It was the largest funeral ever seen in Boston.

According to the Boston papers, Archbishop (now Cardinal) Richard J. Cushing had flown from Washington to deliver the eulogy. The late Cardinal O'Connell had spoken one when Curley's first wife died; the Archbishop himself had eulogized Mary and Leo eight years before. Now he sat silent and dominant in the sanctuary. The celebrant was Curley's youngest son, Father Francis Curley, S.J.

The coffin of polished mahogany glittered in the candlelight that was reflected again on the scabbards of the Knights of Columbus, Fourth Class, who formed the guard of honor. They stood there, plump and middle-aged, in silk capes, their hands on their sword hilts, white plumes covering their heads. As the requiem mass reached its conclusion, the Archbishop approached the coffin. Then he prayed, in the grating, honest, South Boston voice that was his inheritance and that he was too proud to change. High overhead, suspended by a wire from the Reconstruction-Gothic dome and directly over the coffin, Cardinal O'Connell's red hat swung slightly in the air currents.

The prayer ended, and everyone watched the Archbishop's seamed face under its white miter, waiting for him to mount the steps to the pulpit. But the Archbishop did not move. There was no eulogy.

Francis Russell was brought up in the Boston suburb of Dorchester. His Irish great-grandmother came to America in the famine year of 1848. He has written about Irish-Americans in several publications, among them the Irish Digest *and the* Antioch Review, *and is a frequent contributor to* AMERICAN HERITAGE.

The Glorious Unsafe Fourth CONTINUED FROM PAGE 43

was in seeing how close you could come in a race of this sort and still win. One way to do it was to hold the firecracker in one hand while you lit it with the other, and then, just as the fizzing red line of fire reached the fuse's end, to throw it as far as you could. Meanwhile your heart would be pounding so hard that it affected your hearing, and sometimes the firecracker would explode in your hand. As a result of my mother's predictions, I always expected to lose a finger doing this. But I still have them all.

After breakfast we began experimenting with ways of increasing the noise or using the impact of the explosion. The wonderfully stimulating, acrid smell of gunpowder was by now well worked into our clothes. Sometimes, as we bent over a firecracker, the stinging smoke from a stick of punk would get in our eyes. Punk was indispensable. It came in thin sticks, and once lighted would burn slowly and always be at hand for touching off a fuse.

One of our favorite ways of testing the power of our salutes was to set one on a stone or slate, light the fuse, quickly drop a tin can or lard pail on it, and then get out of the way. Then we would try two or three salutes, until we had pails sailing higher than the tallest elms, with a muffled report that shook the heart inside your ribs and set your blood pumping with delight.

My father, who enjoyed the Fourth as much as we did, was especially fond of these can-lifting operations. I can see him now, coming out of the cellar with a small bucket and saying, "Here you are, boys. Let's see what we can do with this." We knew he wanted to shoot a few himself, so with that willingness to indulge a childish parent which is one of childhood's endearing traits, we provided the materials.

He made careful preparations, lighted the fuse, and stepped back. The bucket rose gracefully above the roof, lost momentum, then turned and fell with an aimed precision into the chimney. It later cost him several dollars to get the obstruction removed.

"You'll probably need this for more fireworks," he said, handing me fifty cents. "And I wouldn't say anything to your mother about that bucket. You know how women are about the Fourth."

My mother, as a matter of fact, had bandages and ointments ready for the accidents she had predicted. But my brother and I made it a point of honor never to take our Fourth of July wounds to her.

Sometimes we would rub a little butter on a burn, but burns that would have demanded maternal care on other days never seemed to hurt much on the Fourth. No psychologists, we assumed that the reason lay in some healing power the gunpowder possessed, and never questioned it further.

By mid-morning we were down on Main Street waiting for the parade. On this particular Fourth we also had a human fly who was going to climb up the outside of our local skyscraper—a six-story building with a fancy cornice on which he proposed to ride a bicycle.

The human fly came every year, but this was the first time he had come on the Fourth. For weeks after his performances, we would imitate his methods on house and barn until a sprained ankle or a turned wrist ended our enthusiasm. But the bicycle stunt was new, and it drew a large crowd.

The ease with which he got up the face of the building was amazing, but when he balanced his bicycle on that swooping cornice, we were in an ecstasy of excitement, not quite sure whether we wanted him to succeed or preferred to be present at his gruesome demise. How he managed to mount and get momentum without tumbling off I still do not know. There was in it that element of danger that belonged to the Fourth.

Shortly after his act was over, we could hear the tentative drumbeats and horn-warmings of the band assembling at the monument square. Then, after a long wait, the first line of the parade came down the hill. It consisted, as always, of our four biggest cops, dressed in long coats that they filled out in a magnificent parabola from chin to thigh. Then the flags, then the Civil War veterans, still more than a dozen of them, dressed in their blue uniforms and campaign hats with the golden cords.

They got a big hand, but when the young men from the recent war (we were not quite sure what to call it then, though many favored "the European War" or "the Great War") came stepping along in their high-collared uniforms with knee breeches and rolled puttees, they got a rousing welcome. To us they were the ones who had licked the Huns and put the Kaiser in his place and shown Europe what stuff Americans were made of.

After them came George Drum's band, a semiprofessional outfit that gave concerts in the bandstand Saturday nights. The tuba player always attracted me most. He seemed to have a note for each foot that he played as he put that foot forward—oom-pah, oom-pah—in a pattern that never varied. Under the broiling sun his round face was bathed in sweat, and drops of water ran down his cheeks to drip off the point of his chin.

Someone lit a package of small crackers and tossed it neatly into the tuba. The player seemed to be making too much noise himself to hear the explosions, but when smoke began to filter out through his drooping mustache, he stopped to investigate. The crowd was delighted.

Then came floats covered with bunting and representing various ideas of America triumphant; then the Boy Scouts—I could have marched with them but it was more fun to toss firecrackers at their feet. And then, best of all, a Scotch bagpipe band. There was something wild and primitive about their skirling that appealed to a boy's ear, something stirring and rousing and appropriate to the Fourth. The bass drummer was an artist, a whole show in himself. He crossed his arms and tossed his sticks in the air and never missed a beat. Of the several things I would have liked to be, that drummer was first.

A line of new cars ended the parade. There was an Apperson "Jack Rabbit," a Chalmers with a body as big as a whaleboat, a Stanley Steamer quietly hissing, an air-cooled Franklin with its comic-looking hood, and, of course, the plebeian Chevrolet and Maxwell and the indestructible T-model Ford. We knew all these cars by heart and called their names as they passed. Most of them, of course, were touring cars. The swing to sedans was just beginning.

A miscellaneous lot of cars and horse-drawn vehicles followed the parade—high, boxlike milk wagons, ice trucks covered like Conestoga wagons, a baker's truck with rows of drawers, and open delivery wagons. None of them was streamlined, but they were built to fill the special needs they served, and they had a variety in appearance which, as you look back from an assembly-line age, was homely, familiar, and pleasing. Best of all we liked the ice truck, for there were always shards and slivers of ice when the iceman split up the big cakes with his axe. For these we would run behind the cart, calling, "Give us a piece of ice, mister?"

Best of all impromptu excitements was the runaway which invariably occurred on the Fourth. This time it happened just after the parade had passed—a thunder of hoofs, a volley of shouts, and a crowd of running men. The horse turned a sudden corner, the buggy he was pulling smashed against the granite curb and upset, the traces snapped, and the horse lit out for home.

The beauty of his running, free from the load he drew—legs lifted high, mane flying, tail stuck out behind—seemed like the perfect expression of that freedom from restraint that the Fourth meant to a boy.

There was only one dark spot in the day's program—the Fourth of July oration. This year the speaker was our school principal. As he stood up in the bandstand we knew that once he was wound up he might go on for an hour. Yet it never occurred to us to walk out. He was part of the day's ritual. Ordinarily, the best we could hope for to break the monotony was a dog fight. But on this Fourth a special blessing occurred. Somehow—it could have been arranged—a dog and cat found themselves together under the bandstand. Between the platform and the ground was a continuous row of slats intended, no doubt, to keep out dogs and cats. However they had got in there, neither of them was able to get out. Their dispute over the territory, coming at the climax of the oration, was well timed. First a growl, then a frantic barking, then the spitting and spluttering of the cat, then a yowl, then a muffled symphony of noises rising to a shriek, then the injured surprise expressed in a plaintive yip, then the whole round repeated again—we got the whole story by ear. By the time someone had found a way to let the cat out, the orator was floundering in the wreck of his overweighted verbal edifice, the audience was snickering, and the band struck up "The Star-Spangled Banner" in an effort to save the sadly deteriorating situation.

After the noonday dinner there was a ball game, but I didn't go. The afternoon heat settled over us like a thick blanket, leaving us limp and lazy. Now and then a faint breath of air stirred under the trees on the back lawn. We lay around on the grass, tossing a firecracker now and then, resting up for the evening program. Then I persuaded my mother to make us some lemonade, and in honor of the occasion she made it pink. What virtue the color had I do not know, but we assumed that it made an infinitely superior product. The bittersweet flavor clung to the throat; the lumps of ice floating in the glasses made the liquid so cold that we could feel the shock like ice laid at our foreheads when we drank. Then, lying on the soft, cool lawn, we looked up through the rich tangle of leaves, bright green where the sun shone through them and touched with gold at the edges, enjoying the apathy produced by the heat, savoring the delightful prospect of the long, school-free summer that we knew lay ahead of us.

After supper there was another round of activity, beginning with a carnival that included such attractions as the man whose heart was exposed to view, a snake charmer, "real" Hawaiian dancers whom we referred to as "hootchie-cootchies," a Ferris wheel, a merry-go-round, snap-the-whip, chamber of surprises, and a whole row of booths where you could buy something to eat or take a chance or try your skill in a variety of ways.

Money by this time was running short; we had to choose from all these temptations two or three. I chose a hot dog, a cone full of pink spun sugar—cottony stuff that dissolved into sweetness on the tongue—and the chamber of surprises, where I fell down collapsing stairways, looked at myself in rippled mirrors, and spun around on revolving floors.

The carnival brought to our quiet town-life a kind of gaudy splendor and activity that were a welcome change. The shouts of the barkers, the horrible painted canvases advertising the two-headed man and the man-eating savage from Borneo, the rows of tawdry prizes, the confusion of sounds, smells, movement, and garish lighting—all these suggested a possible world wider and brighter than the one we lived in, yet they also established in a subtle way the solid dependability of our own.

By nine thirty it was dark enough for the fireworks exhibit to begin. This was announced by two or three aerial bombs bursting with such magnificent strength that we could feel them in our chests and throats. As amateurs, we appreciated the professional excellence of those explosions. We ran to the edge of the ball field where the set pieces had been put up, their skeletal shapes showing dimly in the dark.

The pieces were mostly patriotic. There was an airplane with a pinwheel whirling around for a propeller. Uncle Sam rode in a car with revolving wheels. As the pieces were set off one after another against the velvet backdrop of the night, the burning colors with their deep pure shades had a quieting effect on us. It was as if we had been initiated into some mystery of beauty whose meaning we did not understand. Each time a piece was set off a chorused "Ah-h-h" came from the watchers—quiet, spontaneous, like the voice of the ocean.

Then an aerial bomb would burst over our heads in an umbrella of colored flowers. And at the end an American flag appeared in full and glowing color, a barrage of bombs exploded in little bursts of light above us, echoing up and down the surrounding hills, and the display was over.

But there was one event still to come. We had our own night pieces to shoot off. Because our yard was large, friends brought their stuff over, the neighbors collected, and we had another celebration. Pinwheels, Roman candles, flower pots, sparklers, fire fountains, and skyrockets—we had them all. Knowing that the sparks from the sparklers were harmless, we liked to hold our hands out to be bombarded by this magic fire that did not burn. Otherwise, we considered sparklers rather tame and sissy. As for the Roman candles, my brother was always pointing them at the crowd in his excitement and causing sudden alarums and excursions.

With a fine disregard for fire hazards, we also sent up hot-air balloons, carrying their own bit of candle to keep them buoyant. I remember them rising in the darkness, their red paper glowing in the dark, floating and bobbing about like buoys in a harbor until they were out of sight.

But best of all were the skyrockets, because they were the most dangerous. We placed them in a wooden trough that was aimed at the open space between the tall elms, just over our barn roof. But skyrockets had a somewhat mulish disposition. They made a great sputter before moving up the trough, and sometimes they burned without taking off at all, or went where they were not expected.

The principal of our school was one of our neighbors, and I suppose he thought it was with premeditated malice that one of our rockets chose to go after him. It chased him around the yard and ran him up a steep bank in a way that was gratifying to see. It was a perfect conclusion to a Glorious Fourth.

With the laws against fireworks and the arrival of radio and allegedly sophisticated forms of entertainment to supplant the human fly, the parade, and the oration, the Glorious Fourth has ceased to be a part of our national life. Maybe it is for the best, since accidents inevitably resulted from the presence of so much gunpowder in eager hands. Yet if we have learned anything in recent years we have learned that danger is inseparable from living.

In any case, no one old enough to remember such a Fourth of July is likely to forget, as long as he lives, the excitement of the dawn awakening, the wonderful pungent smell of gunpowder filling the air, the unaccustomed leniency of parents, the mood of a young nation innocently exulting in its strength and freedom, the glitter of the carnival, the beauty of colored flame burning against the great backdrop of night.

Bradford Smith of Shaftsbury, Vermont, is the author of many works on the American past, including biographies, novels, children's books, and such social histories as Why We Behave Like Americans.

New York's Bloodiest Week

CONTINUED FROM PAGE 49

tan war horse of grizzled locks and martial figure," as one paper described him. Carpenter, promising "to win this fight or never come back alive," led his main force up Broadway with two parallel columns of fifty men ready to strike from the side streets. The police caught the mob by surprise. "Men fell by the dozens under the sturdy blows of the police who had orders to 'take no prisoners,'" the *Times* reported. ". . . Broadway looked like a battleground thickly strewn with prostrate forms."

Another mob, meanwhile, had invaded the *Tribune* building across the park from City Hall. Acton had decided to make his second major attack. He combined a force of almost fifty men at City Hall with the first-precinct reserves and rushed them to the *Tribune* building. Then he ordered Carpenter's men to catch the rioters from the rear.

"We struck them like a thunder-bolt," one officer recalled later. The floors were heaped with bleeding rioters. Hundreds, fleeing down side streets, were caught by Carpenter. "It was a striking illustration of the cowardice of the mob when confronted by a handful of determined officers of the law," the *Times* exulted the next morning. More important, it had not only saved the *Tribune*, *Times*, and *Post* buildings from destruction but demonstrated that the police still controlled the lower city.

That night New York was in turmoil. A Negro cartman, trying to escape under cover of darkness, was caught by a gang of of men and boys and hanged from one of the fine spreading chestnut trees on Clarkson Street. Only a few feet from the consecrated ground of St. John's Cemetery, they built a fire under him, dancing wildly around the roasting flesh.

Shortly after midnight, a deluge of rain drove the rioters temporarily from the streets. At 1:15 A.M. the indefatigable Inspector Carpenter set out with a small force to cut down the body of the Negro cartman. Then Acton received a message, warning of a new attack on police headquarters. Carpenter had to bring back his men.

Tuesday was hot and muggy; a heavy pall of black smoke rose from innumerable fires hanging over the city. Mobs filled the streets at dawn "increasing in power and audacity," noted Ellen Leonard, a young New Englander staying at her brother's house on Nineteenth Street.

News from Gettysburg sharpened the tension. Decisively beaten in the three-day battle there, General Robert E. Lee had withdrawn his battered army and on the night of July 13 had crossed the Potomac and gained comparative safety in Virginia. Northern jubilation over the victory was sharply tempered by the realization that Lee's army had, after all, escaped destruction, and when the government ordered New York National Guard regiments returned from Pennsylvania to New York City to deal with the riot it was commonly assumed that this played directly into Lee's hands. Actually, the escape had already taken place; the National Guard regiments had seen little combat service in the Gettysburg campaign, and their departure did not deprive the Union commander, General George G. Meade, of any essential support once the Confederates had gone south of the Potomac. Nevertheless, the fact that Union troops had to be sent to New York at a time when a dangerous Confederate army still needed attention was profoundly dismaying, and the *Times*, not surprisingly, declared editorially that the New York rioters were "the left wing of Lee's army."

Although some reporters considered the mob a directionless rabble, others noted disturbing signs of organization—the well-constructed barricades, for example, on First Avenue between Eleventh and Fourteenth streets, used as fortress and virtual assembly-ground by the mob.

John Andrews was still supplying leadership on the East Side. Ellen Leonard saw him on horseback that morning, noting that "crowds quickly gathered around him . . . from all the neighboring alleys and greeted him with shouts and cheers." The *Times* added, "We have not a doubt there are other men, agents direct from Richmond, now in the city . . ." When the police later tried to identify one of the most daring mob leaders killed on Second Avenue, and found under his grimy work clothes a handsome vest and an expensive linen shirt, the suspicions seemed justified.

Pitched battles, even more furious than Monday's, raged all day. A company of soldiers faced one mob at point-blank range on Delancey Street, fought them off, and was attacked again on Pitt Street. A marine detachment was forced to retreat before another mob on Grand Street. Almost 5,000 rioters invaded the Union Steam Works at 22nd Street and Second Avenue, where thousands of government carbines were stored. A strong force of police under Inspector George Dilks stormed the building, piled the carbines on wagons, and marched quickly downtown to relieve Mayor Opdyke's house, which was under attack. Meanwhile

Commissioner Thomas Acton

Police Chief John Kennedy

Fire Chief John Decker

Inspector Dan Carpenter

the mob retook the Steam Works, and Dilks had to return and fight for it again, floor by floor.

Inspector Carpenter with 300 police battled a mob estimated at 10,000 on Second Avenue. In phalanx formation the police hammered their way through the rioters. But at 34th Street they stepped into a trap. Hundreds of rioters, placed on rooftops and in windows, picked off the police with guns and bricks. Colonel Henry O'Brien offered to rush a detachment of his Eleventh New York Volunteers, a new regiment still being organized, to clear the avenue with two field-pieces while Carpenter's men methodically routed the rioters from each building.

Colonel O'Brien, who lived on Second Avenue near 35th Street, soon paid for his daring. An Irishman himself, he foolishly assumed that his name would protect him from retribution and returned home alone a few hours later, stopping at a neighborhood drugstore. A crowd quickly gathered outside the store. O'Brien stepped out boldly, sword in one hand, pistol in the other. A woman hurled a brick, he fired, and then the mob swallowed him up, beating him, the *Tribune* reported, with "every club that could be brought to bear, every kick or stone that could be thrown . . ." He was dragged, still breathing, over the rough cobblestones to his own courtyard, where for hours women and boys, as well as men, danced around the body. They paused only to allow a priest to administer the last rites. When a neighboring druggist offered the dying man a glass of water, his store was sacked.

That same morning Governor Seymour arrived from Long Branch, New Jersey. From City Hall, after conferring with Opdyke, he issued a strong proclamation calling for the restoration of law and order. Then a large crowd gathered in the park, and Seymour went to the steps of City Hall to address them—a speech that has remained the most controversial act of his controversial career.

"Let me assure you that I am your friend," he told his listeners. "You have been my friends. And now I assure you, my fellow citizens, that I am here to show you a test of my friendship. I wish to inform you that I have sent my Adjutant General to Washington to confer with the authorities there and to have this draft suspended and stopped . . ."

Seymour's supporters have always claimed his first responsibility was to calm the city—that nothing more was implied in his words. But Administration papers bristled at this offer of "friendship" and obvious appeasement of the rioters. "He was proclaiming with all the authority attaching to his character and official position," stated the *Times*, "that mob law ought under certain circumstances to over-ride that of Congress. . . ."

Mayor Opdyke now was harassed both by Seymour and the Peace Democrats who controlled his own Board of Aldermen and City Council. While Seymour was speaking, the aldermen and council were preparing a $2,500,000 Conscription Exemption Bond bill which would allow the city to give $300 to each drafted man to buy his way out of the service. They passed the bill on Wednesday, and Opdyke immediately vetoed it, stating, "I felt it would be purchasing the peace of the city too dearly to thus bow to dictation of the mob. . . ."

The real struggle was at the barricades on Eighth Avenue between 37th and 43rd streets and on First Avenue between Eleventh and Fourteenth streets. Commissioner Acton and General Brown combined strong forces of soldiers and police, and by midnight took the barricades. But fighting went on all night.

From her room Ellen Leonard watched the rioters still surging through Nineteenth Street and noted that her "neighborhood was wholly at the mercy of the mob . . . Destruction and death were on every side." She tried to sleep "when a sudden rush and scream brought me again to my window . . . I distinctly heard dreadful cries and caught these broken words, 'Oh my brothers! My brothers! Save me!'"

Not many hours afterward, on Wednesday afternoon, Ellen Leonard and her household were to play a heroic role in one of the decisive battles of the week. That morning a mob of 5,000 had been cleared from Seventh Avenue and 32nd Street by a force of U.S. artillery firing grape at point-blank range and killing scores of rioters. But the mob collected again in greater strength at Nineteenth Street and First Avenue. Colonel Cleveland Winslow, with one of the few small infantry detachments available for street-fighting, and Colonel Edward Jardine, with a battery of two howitzers, marched to meet them.

As Winslow's men rushed forward, they were attacked from every window and rooftop by rifle fire and bricks. The infantry was cut to pieces. Winslow had to order an immediate retreat. Jardine, struck by a bullet in the leg, crumpled to the pavement.

The regimental surgeon helped Colonel Jardine and another wounded soldier escape down Nineteenth Street. Ellen saw them from her window. She rushed downstairs and begged them to take refuge in the house. The Colonel and the surgeon were hidden in the cellar, the soldier taken to the top floor where Ellen and her mother could nurse him. Ellen's brother was sent for help, escaping over the rooftops at the rear. "Mrs. P.," who lived downstairs, waited calmly in the sitting room.

The rioters were combing the street, house by house. "A few moments we waited in breathless silence," Ellen wrote later. "Then came a rush up the stairs and the bell rang violently." The mob demanded that the soldiers be given up. Mrs. P. answered them calmly. Yes, they had been here, but had escaped by the back yard. One man pointed a carbine at her head. She brushed it aside, saying, "You know I am a woman, and it might frighten me." They threatened to burn the house down. "My only son works as you do, and perhaps in the same shop with some of you, for seventy cents a day," she told them, omitting the fact that he had left a few weeks before to join the Union Army.

The sentinel at the stairs, younger and better dressed than the others, drew Mrs. P. aside and warned her that it was better to let them search the house. She agreed, trying to remain calm while they rushed to the cellar. They found the surgeon first and dragged him upstairs, beating him viciously. But Colonel Jardine, lying wounded on the cellar floor, insisted he was an ordinary citizen accidentally hurt in the fray.

Four men pointed muskets at his head. He told them to shoot—he would be dead soon from loss of blood anyway. But he begged them to bring a priest first. The request seemed to disconcert them. Then they left the house as suddenly as they had come, not even bothering to search the upper floors.

The women waited fearfully all that evening. Not until after midnight did they hear the welcome tramp of marching feet. Ellen's brother had reached police headquarters, and returned with a large contingent of soldiers and police. The whole party was rescued and taken to the well-guarded St. Nicholas Hotel. Even the surgeon, they learned, had managed to escape.

In the early hours of Thursday morning, the mob attacked a government warehouse on Greenwich Street, where 20,000 muskets were stored. This cache might have given them control of the city if Acton had not learned of the plan in time and sent a large headquarters force to stop them.

It was almost dawn before the turning point arrived. The steady tramp of thousands of feet—the Tenth and Fifty-sixth regiments, New York National Guard—was heard along lower Broadway. At 4 A.M. the perfectly formed ranks of the crack Seventh Regiment wheeled up Canal Street. They were the first elements of the state militia rushed from Gettysburg. Nine more New York regiments as well as one Michigan regiment arrived in the next two days. The city was out of danger at last.

From Washington on Thursday the President announced that he was standing firm: the draft would be resumed in New York at the first practicable date. Late that morning a detachment of police broke into No. 10 East Eleventh Street and arrested John Andrews, "this

Mayor George Opdyke

Archbishop John Hughes

Congressman Fernando Wood

Governor Horatio Seymour

howling fiend, this emissary and spy of the Rebels," as the *Tribune* called him, who ironically enough was found with his Negro mistress.

The mob was to make its last stand on the East Side. Five thousand desperate men attacked elements of the Seventh Regiment on Second Avenue in what the *Times* labeled "the most sanguinary fight of the whole riot." Bullets and bricks from the rooftops killed fifteen soldiers before another 700 troops arrived to clear the avenue with artillery and bayonet.

I t was the decisive battle. On Friday morning, the Mayor could announce: "The riotous assemblages have been dispersed."

On Friday, also, John Hughes, Roman Catholic Archbishop of New York, made an address from the balcony of his house at 36th Street and Madison Avenue. A loyal supporter of the Union, he had traveled in Europe as Lincoln's personal agent, speaking for the Union cause in Rome, France, and Ireland. He had no love for abolitionists, but he did not like mob rule either, and on Thursday it had been announced that he would address "the men of New York who are now called in many of the papers rioters." The wording of this proclamation disturbed the New York *Times,* which wondered what other term could be applied to men who had burned down public buildings, but the speech was a firm one, and it served to tamp down the last embers of revolt.

While the riots disappeared from the headlines by the end of the week, their repercussions continued. The President appointed Major General John A. Dix, former governor of New York, to the eastern command, and set August 19 as the date for the resumption of the draft. But Seymour was intractable. In letter after letter he argued with Lincoln that the city's quotas had been unfairly set, that prejudiced officials would corrupt the drawing, that he could fill New York's quotas immediately with volunteers. Lincoln rejected each excuse patiently but firmly. The draft was completed —but at some expense to the campaign against Lee.

"As it is quite possible we may be obliged to detach some of your troops to enforce the draft and to bring on the drafted men," General in Chief Henry W. Halleck wired General George G. Meade, commander of the Army of the Potomac, on July 29, "I think it would be best to hold for the present the upper line of the Rappahannock without further pursuit of Lee." The necessity had to be met, and Meade told Halleck on August 16, "I have sent you my best troops and some of my best officers"—almost 10,000 soldiers from the Army of the Potomac.

Firm as he had been with Seymour, Lincoln squashed all attempts to link the New York riots and leading Peace Democrats with Richmond. When James R. Gilmore of the New York *Tribune* called on Lincoln and proposed an investigation of the riot's causes, the President refused, supposedly saying, "One rebellion at a time is about as much as we can conveniently handle."

The ironic conclusion to the riots was the 1863 draft itself. Of 79,975 men conscripted in New York State, 54,765 were exempted on physical and other grounds, 15,912 bought their way out for $300, 6,998 furnished substitutes, and only 2,300—not many more than had been killed and wounded in the riots themselves— were added to the Union Army. In the North as a whole, in fact, the four drafts of 1863 and 1864 produced about 52,000 troops.

Yet the value of conscription could not be measured solely by the number of men drafted. Each state was given a quota at each call for troops, and officials tried to meet the quotas ahead of time by swelling their voluntary enlistments. So the threat of a draft was an invaluable asset as a constant prod. States and cities that raised more than their share of men could credit the extras to their quota at the time of the next draft.

There was a further irony in the attention focused by the riots on the $300 exemption clause. During the debates on a new draft law early in 1864, a large block of senators and congressmen opposed the exemption as "class legislation." Lincoln himself, with an election only a few months off, joined the opposition in June, thus daring the political wrath of those in wealth and power who supported the exemption. The final bill, passed on July 4, established a new system of bounty payments in graduated amounts for one-year, two-year, and three-year volunteers.

But when the $300 exemption came to a vote, both Fernando and Ben Wood, the most frenzied opponents of the exemption as a crime against the poor, refrained from voting!

And to add to the complex irony, the War Department during the fall, 1864, draft was so intent on placating New York that 18,448 men who had enlisted in the Navy during the four preceding years were credited to the city. Thus was its quota virtually filled by paper logistics. Thus did sailors from Iowa or Michigan, who happened to have signed their Navy papers in New York, keep the specter of another draft riot from a city that had already known the worst explosion in the nation's history.

Lawrence Lader of New York City is a veteran free-lance writer and a former president of the Society of Magazine Writers. He is now at work on a study of the antislavery movement in New England before the Civil War, to be published next year by E. P. Dutton.

READING, WRITING, AND HISTORY

*When the American republic was still young, and seemed in the European view to be
a daring experiment that might or might not come to anything, Alexis de Tocqueville
visited these shores and wrote a book,* Democracy in America, *which was accepted then
and afterward as a brilliant examination of this strange new society. It remains a classic
in its field; and now, a full century after its author's death, a re-examination of what its
author really had to say is very much in order.*

Accordingly, in this space which is ordinarily reserved for reviews of current books,
AMERICAN HERITAGE *in this issue turns to a consideration of Tocqueville and his message—a message which is as relevant today, in the time of this nation's maturity, as it was
when it was first written. This article was written by J. A. Lukacs, author of* The European
Revolution *and professor of history at Chestnut Hill and La Salle Colleges, Philadelphia.*

DE TOCQUEVILLE'S MESSAGE FOR AMERICA

Alexis de Tocqueville died a hundred years ago, on
April 16, 1859, after years of increasing suffering,
with his gloomy neurotic wife at his side, in a villa
on a hill above Cannes. At that time Cannes and the
Riviera were not yet fashionable places. The Tocque-
villes had gone there from the foggy *brume* of Nor-
mandy, to profit from the Mediterranean air. It was
of no use. His chest was ravaged beyond repair. Thus
he succumbed, to be buried quietly in an unpreten-
tious tomb tight against the wall of the parish church
in the tiny village of Tocqueville, on the road from
Valognes to Cherbourg, a couple of miles inland from
the English Channel. The marble has already grayed
and some of the letters are hardly legible now.

One mile to the east lies the Tocqueville château.
It is a very French château, with a very Norman court-

yard. At least part of one wing, holding a tiny chapel,
goes back to the fifteenth century. There is an enormous square pile of concrete, an abandoned German
bunker, in the middle of the fields. The château was
headquarters for a German military command, and
the bunker is a leftover reminder of Hitler's Atlantic
"wall." The cost of its removal would be exorbitant.
Ahead of the courtyard there is a partly weedy pond,
and the main part of the château is gutted by fire.
Four years ago, when the present Comte de Tocqueville, a lateral descendant, was making some repairs,
a blowtorch started a blaze and the central part
burned out.

Yet the best room in the château, Alexis de Tocqueville's erstwhile library, was saved in a miraculous way.
It is a dark, big room, with a magnificent tapestry,

Alexis de Tocqueville's ancestral home was a typically Norman château on the Channel coast near Cherbourg.

packed full to the top with books and papers and folders; almost incredibly, that very mass of tightly packed papers somehow refused to catch fire. The flames stopped at the doorway; it is as if they had hesitated, blowing and licking around that portal until they turned their fiery wrath elsewhere.

So the library stands there now, nearly intact, with Tocqueville's own books, with perhaps the only portrait of their master on the wall. There are a few bills and accounts and some correspondence relating to the Tocqueville papers on the desk still used on occasion by Alexis' descendants. I felt a faint sense of latent life in that dark room. It was as if the master of the room had been away, on a long and perilous journey but, still, perhaps on his way back . . .

This is a personal impression of a personal feeling. Yet it is symbolic in at least one sense. It is symbolic of Tocqueville's century-long round trip in the memory of mankind.

A hundred years ago his death stirred not many people. By 1859 Tocqueville had already been near the end of what amounted to a decade of almost complete retirement from public affairs. A few weeks after his death a great European crisis flared up into war not very far from Cannes. In the United States, too, the rumblings of that tragic year 1859 were not conducive to philosophic contemplations about Tocqueville. Most of his American friends were dead by that time. Thus the decline of his reputation continued.

For at least sixty years Tocqueville was largely forgotten. In the United States the two heavy volumes of Lord Bryce on *The American Commonwealth* overshadowed Tocqueville's reputation. In the thirty years after its first publication, thirty American editions of *Democracy in America* had appeared; in the next sixty years their number falls to thirteen. In England the respective numbers are seven and three; in France, thirteen and four.

This was consequent to the political atmosphere of late Victorianism. Between 1865 and 1914 liberalism and industrial democracy grew rapidly throughout the Western World. The prevailing bent of thought was pragmatic. The prevailing political categories were still "liberal" and "conservative," but the very meanings of these words had begun to change.

Somehow Tocqueville did not fit into either of these categories. How could he be a liberal, he who had warned people so often against putting too much faith into optimistic concepts of sinless human nature, and who had expressed many doubts about such concepts as evolution or industrial progress? And was he a "true" conservative, he who had warned people that they would do better to understand and acquiesce in democracy since, in one form or another, it was here to stay?

At times, when he was not forgotten at all, Tocqueville was regarded as an archaic, aristocratic, sententious thinker, a "conservative liberal" or a "liberal conservative" of the receding past. A few decades after his death, the author of a Parisian comedy, *Le monde ou l'on s'ennuie,* made the audience smirk as the stiff and ambitious little provincial wife introduced one of her statements with the words: *"comme disait M. de Tocqueville"*—"as M. de Tocqueville said."

Yet there were exceptions. They stand out today, in retrospect. Our generation has begun to rediscover not only Tocqueville but Acton and Burckhardt and Dicey and Dilthey and Droysen among the greatest historical thinkers of the past hundred years; it is significant that during their lifetime all of these men, independently of each other, discovered and admired Tocqueville. His name crops up, here and there, from their notes. Acton, who at first frets uneasily about Tocqueville, ends up by jotting down: "One cannot find fault with him. He is as just as Aristides." Thirty-odd years ago a lonely and brooding Frenchman, M. Antoine Redier, began to be intrigued by Tocqueville; he read his books, looked into his papers, traced the last years of his life, and arrived at the, at first, astonishing conclusion that here was perhaps the greatest thinker of the past three or four centuries. Appropriately enough, he entitled his little book *Comme Disait M. de Tocqueville.*

The book is out of print now. It still failed to stir many people in France in the 1920's. It was from the hot ashes of German ruin that Tocqueville's memory began to rise again during our own lifetime. The spectacle of a Hitler coming to power largely through the democratic process belatedly awakened many minds to the realization that here was something new—or, rather, that it was the very danger that Tocqueville had first described: the tyranny of the majority, a democratic possibility that the accepted liberal categories of thought had refused to admit at all.

Meanwhile, in America the intellectual enthusiasm generated during the first period of the New Deal was wearing thin as many liberals themselves learned how the vulgar exploitation of majority sentiment may prove to be a great danger to free democracies. It is for this reason that, ever since the end of the last war, Tocqueville has gained a new American reputation. An excellent full edition of *Democracy in America* was published in 1945; the next thirteen years saw perhaps a dozen new editions and paperbacks, not only of *Democracy in America* but also of the *Recollections* and of the *Old Regime and the Revolution.* Nowadays there is hardly a month in which one of our more serious columnists or commentators on public affairs does not cite some pertinent Tocquevillean passage. Meanwhile in France, with the assistance of the Rockefeller Foundation, the first complete edition of Tocqueville's collected works has begun under the editorship of a devoted scholar, J. P. Mayer.

Of course, the Tocquevillean heritage is a very large one. The full edition of his papers may run to more than twenty volumes, most of it correspondence, and very valuable letters these are indeed. There is hardly a dull page in them. For one thing, they deal with an extraordinary variety of themes: religion, politics, philosophy, race, economics, literature, the tendency of manners, sexual morality, Asia, Russia, India. . . . For another matter, Tocqueville was a superb stylist. He furnishes us with a potential mine of quotations. It would be easy to string some of them together, taking them from *Democracy in America* alone, to impress every reader with the pertinent wisdom of a great prophet.

For Tocqueville predicted not only the possibility of majoritarian tyranny but almost every one of its actual and potential dangers. He predicted, among other things, the Civil War, the extinction of the Indians, the lasting character of the Negro problem, the future population of the Union, the coming shape of American public education, juvenile delinquency due to the loosening of parental authority, the future of American Catholicism, the coming ascendancy of America and Russia over most of the world.

It is always tempting to quote all of that now famous paragraph which concludes the first volume of *Democracy in America,* about a future America and a future Russia, one standing for freedom, the other for servitude; "their starting-point is different and their courses are not the same; yet each of them seems marked out by the will of Heaven to sway the destinies of half the globe."

Now consider only how this country has changed since 1831. When Tocqueville was here, he saw a powerful but still limited republic, at the edge of the Western World, its energies directed away from Europe, still committed to the toleration of slavery, with a uniquely limited federal bureaucracy, without much of a standing army, with a population that was almost exclusively Protestant and the overwhelming majority of which had come or descended from the inhabitants of the British Isles (Tocqueville called them Anglo-Americans throughout). Today this country has become the most powerful nation in the world, ready to conquer the moon, with military bases in fifty countries throughout the globe, carrying a principal voice in the affairs of Europe, committed against slavery, maintaining military establishments to the amount of about fifty billion dollars a year, with a governmental bureaucracy of enormous proportions, a nation whose population is no longer predominantly Anglo-Saxon in its origins, and where there is even a tendency toward a Catholic majority.

The contrast is tremendous. How come, then, that almost everything Tocqueville wrote about Jackson's America in 1831–1832 is still so true about this very different America today? How come that we may open Tocqueville's book, written 125 years ago, at virtually any page and find passages that are directly and clearly pertinent to the problems of the United States today?

The answer, I think, lies in a quality of Tocqueville's which has been seldom mentioned at all. It is that Tocqueville fully recognized what may be called a change in the texture of history. It would not be an

Alexis de Tocqueville, after the Chassériau etching.

exaggeration to say that he was the first historian of the democratic age. For we must consider that though proclamations of the ideals of political democracy are marked on crucial milestones in the history of the past four or five centuries, the full extent of majority rule did not affect the nations of the Western World until almost our very lifetime. Jacksonian America was an early example of such a national society. And the task which Tocqueville had set for himself was "to penetrate beneath accidental history to solid history, or beneath history to the physiology of peoples."

This is how his ungenerous critic, Émile Faguet, put it sixty years ago; but Faguet was critical of that self-imposed task. Yet this is why the value of Tocqueville's work is so permanent. Contrary to the general assumption, his purpose was not a book about America but about this new kind of democracy, for the sake of France and of Europe. And there is, for once, a seldom-cited passage from *Democracy in America* which our statesmen in Washington would do well to ponder today:

Those who, after having read this book, should imagine that my intention in writing it was to propose the laws and customs of the Anglo-Americans for the imitation of all democratic communities would make a great mistake; they must have paid more attention to the form than to the substance of my thought. My aim has been to show, by the example of America, that laws, and especially customs, may allow a democratic people to remain free. But I am very far from thinking that we ought to follow the example of the American democracy and copy the means that it has employed to attain this end; for I am well aware of the influence which the nature of a country and its political antecedents exercise upon its political constitution; and I should regard it as a great misfortune for mankind if liberty were to exist all over the world under the same features.

For *Democracy in America* is, in more than one sense, a still unexplored book. Especially the second volume, filled with daring generalizations, is seldom being read through; its implications have seldom been studied with any great effort of concentration. Nor is our knowledge of Tocqueville the man very extensive.

Except for the brilliant short introductory biographies by Redier and Mayer, little has been written about his life. True, his personal history may not have been exceptionally dramatic: his wife, a middle-class Englishwoman, was not very attractive; he never belonged to a cohesive political group; his public career was spasmodic; he spent the last part of his life in self-imposed retirement from the world; he died at the age of 54. We have few pictures of him; there is no photograph or daguerreotype. There is the drawing by Chassériau, showing a serious aristocratic mien, a

delicate expression combined with a strong look from those exceptionally perceptive eyes. The oil portrait in the château is rather poor. We know that he was a small, bony man, suffering from a pulmonary disease. An American visitor at the Paris Embassy once made fun of the sudden agitation of his English speech, which seemed so inconsistent, coming out with so much fire from the mouth of this little Frenchman.

Even though a renewed interest in Tocqueville has now taken place, our knowledge and our understanding of him may still be superficial. We have only begun to recognize the rich depth of his writings; and our understanding is still hindered by the automatic application of inadequate categories to his thought. He is regarded a sociologist when, in reality, he was a historian—but a new kind of historian. If this is not evident from *Democracy in America*, where his treatment is, of course, not chronological, it should be certainly evident from his *Old Regime and the Revolution*. People regard him as an aristocrat who criticized democracy when, in reality, he was critical of many aristocratic pretensions and he saw the will of God in the coming democratic age.

"I have always said," he wrote in one of his finest personal letters, "that it is more difficult to stabilize and maintain liberty in our new democratic societies than in certain aristocratic societies of the past. But I shall never dare think it impossible. And I pray to God lest He inspire me with the idea that one may as well despair of trying."

Tocqueville's greatness is latent in this very condition: he transcends categories. He was neither an academic sociologist nor a professional historian. Nor is it possible to solve the problem by assigning him into ambiguous categories of a conservative liberal or a liberal conservative. The very temperament of this man was such that he could never rest content with mere compromise, with moderation for moderation's sake. Tocqueville, therefore, is not in the middle of these categories. He transcends both.

From *Democracy in America* alone we should grasp the enduring truth that its author was neither a skeptical aristocrat nor an academic sociologist nor a defeatist conservative but, as Edward Everett put it long ago, the sincerest foreign friend this democracy has yet had. Nor is there any reason to revise now, 120 years later, what perhaps the first American reviewer of Tocqueville's book wrote in the *American Monthly Magazine*. In tracing the causes of American liberty, this anonymous reviewer wrote in 1838, "in examining how far they continue to influence our conduct, manners, and opinions, and in searching for means to prevent their decay or destruction, the intelligent American reader can find no better guide." —*J. A. Lukacs* turn to the Commandments, only this time he is for total repeal. "I often pass before your house. It appears desolate to me. Formerly I broke the Commandment by coveting it along with my neighbor's wife. Now I do not covet it any more, so I am less a sinner. But as to his wife I always find these Commandments inconvenient and I am sorry that they were ever made. If in your travels you happen to see the Holy Father, ask him to repeal them, as things given only to the Jews and too uncomfortable for good Christians."

Marriage in heaven, which she had hinted at, was a prospect so agreeable and theoretical as to call forth all their powers of wit.

In paradise [she writes] we shall be reunited, never to leave each other again! We shall there live on roasted apples only; the music will be composed of Scotch airs; all parties will be given over to chess, so that no one may be disappointed; every one will speak the same language; the English will be neither unjust nor wicked there; the women will not be coquettes, the men will be neither jealous nor too gallant; . . . Every day we shall love one another, in order that we may love one another still more the day after; in a word, we shall be completely happy. In the meantime let us get all the good we can out of this poor world of ours.

He is charmed with her description of paradise and her plan of living there, and wonders how they should arrange their affairs in that country.

Probably more than forty years will elapse after my arrival there before you follow me. I am a little afraid that in the course of such a long period you may forget me. I have therefore thought of proposing that you give me your word of honor not to renew there your contract with Mr. B—. I shall at the same time give you mine that I shall wait for you. But that gentleman is so good, so generous towards us, he loves you so much and we love him, that I cannot think of this proposal without some scruples of conscience. And yet the idea of an eternity in which I shall be favored with no more than permission to kiss your hands, or sometimes your cheeks, and to pass two or three hours in your sweet society on Wednesdays and Saturdays is frightful. . . . I shall have time, during those forty years, to practice on the armonica, and perhaps I shall play well enough to accompany you on your pianoforte. From time to time we shall have little concerts. . . . We shall eat apples of paradise roasted with butter and nutmeg. And we shall pity those who are not dead.

She assures him that if his "French is not very pure, it is at least very clear!" and promises to become his wife in paradise, "on condition, however, that you do not eye too many of the [heavenly] maidens while waiting for me. I want a faithful husband when I take

one for eternity." This celestial conceit was so appealing, in fact, that Franklin employed it the following year in his fruitless wooing of Madame Helvétius.

In the spring of 1782 peace negotiations got under way at the American Embassy in Paris, and Franklin seems not to have written Madame Brillon as often as she wished. From Nice came a formal complaint. She implores Justice to weigh in her "dreaded balance the reciprocal treaties between the Ambassador and the Lady whom he has abused in a cruel manner," sets forth the facts, and concludes: "The petitioner in this cause requires that the said M. Benjamin Franklin be condemned in her favor for all expense, damage, and interest which you [Justice] shall be pleased to determine upon the stated facts."

Prompted by this mock-complaint, he replies after the manner of the preliminary peace treaty with England, on which he was even then hard at work. You, who "would engross all my Affection, and permit me none for the other amiable Ladies of your Country," are unjust "in your Demands, and in the open War you declare against me if I do not comply with them. Indeed it is I that have the most Reason to complain. My poor little Boy [Amor], whom you ought methinks to have cherish'd, instead of being fat and Jolly like those in your elegant Drawings, is meagre and starv'd almost to death for want of the substantial Nourishment which you his Mother inhumanly deny him, and yet would now clip his little Wings to prevent his seeking it elsewhere!"

He therefore proposes a treaty between them. "I fancy we shall neither of us get any thing by this War, and therefore as feeling my self the Weakest, I will do

Benjamin Franklin Playing Armonica, which he invented in 1762

what indeed ought always to be done by the Wisest, be first in making the Propositions for Peace. That a Peace may be lasting, the Articles of the Treaty should be regulated upon the Principles of the most perfect Equity & Reciprocity." Nine articles follow. "Let me know what you think of these Preliminaries," he asks her. "To me they seem to express the true Meaning and Intention of each Party more plainly than most Treaties. . . . I shall insist pretty strongly on the eighth Article ['That when he is with her, he will do what he pleases'], tho' without much Hope of your Consent to it; and on the ninth also ['that he will love any other Woman as far as he finds her amiable'], tho I despair of ever finding any other Woman that I could love with equal Tenderness."

The real war between nations was over at last, and Franklin was anxious to have done with ministerial duties and go home. Not until 1785 did Congress give its consent. For Madame Brillon, who had invested the larger amount of emotional stock in their friendship, it was a painful leave-taking. "Every day of my existence, memory reminds me that a great man, a sage, once deigned to be my friend. . . . if it be sweet for you to recall the woman who loved you most dearly, think of me, think of all those members of my family who were and always must be your best friends." She was happy to learn of his safe arrival at Philadelphia in September but feels keenly the distance which now separates them. "At least recall occasionally the one among your friends who loved you best, and write to her a few lines in what you call your wretched French. For my part, I shall keep you informed concerning a family you once held dear!"

His only letter to her from America, at least the only one that has survived, was prompted in part by the grief she experienced at the death of her husband and oldest grandchild. "I sympathize with you in all your Losses and Afflictions, and hope the rest of your Life will be as tranquil and free from Trouble as it had been for some Years before we parted . . . being

now in my 83d Year, I do not expect to continue much longer a Sojourner in this World, and begin to promise myself much Gratification of my Curiosity in soon visiting some other."

In the spring of 1789—revolution was just four months distant—she writes him for the last time. "I have given thanks to Providence, which, if it be really endowed with that justice one is accustomed to attribute to it, ought to leave you here on earth as an example to mankind and as a model of wisdom, at least to as ripe an old age as that of the patriarch Matusalem." She asks him to pray for France at this "critical stage."

"I revere you, honor you, love you," she continues; "not a day passes that my heart does not draw nigh you at least in thought; not one wherein I fail to recall your friendship, so precious to me that nothing can ever rob me of it, and the memory of the days during which I enjoyed it more closely, more intimately, makes one of the bright spots of happiness in my life." After this letter Madame Brillon passes from view; there is no record, apparently, of what happened to her and her daughters from this time on.

Franklin for his part must have been thinking especially of her when he wrote Madame Lavoisier that he could not "forget Paris, and the nine years' happiness I enjoyed there, in the sweet society of a people whose conversation is instructive, whose manners are highly pleasing, and who, above all the nations of the world, have, in the greatest perfection, the art of making themselves beloved by strangers. And now, even in my sleep, I find, that the scenes of all my pleasant dreams are laid in that city, or in its neighbourhood."

Bruce Ingham Granger teaches English at the University of Oklahoma. This article was written under the auspices of the American Philosophical Society, which now possesses the Franklin-Brillon correspondence. The society will publish the letters in their entirety, edited by Dr. Gilbert Chinard, later this year.

THE PAST IS FEMININE

History is the product of a temperament that delights in the past, and for which the detachment, the immobility, the deadness and the irrelevance of the past are not defects to be removed, but blessed virtues to be enjoyed. . . . The world has no love for what is dead, wishing only to recall it to life again and make it appear relevant to present pursuits and enterprises. It deals with the past as with a man, expecting it to talk sense and to have something apposite to say. But for the "historian" for whom the past is dead and irreproachable, the past is feminine. He loves it as a mistress of whom he never tires, and whom he never expects to talk sense.

MICHAEL OAKESHOTT, IN *History Today*, FEBRUARY, 1959.

Of Raleigh and the First Plantation CONTINUED FROM PAGE 12

this provides one of the tantalizing "ifs" of history; for immediately after they had gone, Raleigh's supply ship turned up, looked for the colonists and, not finding them, returned with her provisions to England. A fortnight after that, Grenville arrived with three ships well-provided. He himself traveled "up into divers places of the country" seeking for news of the colony in vain.

Then, "unwilling to lose the possession of the country which Englishmen had so long held, after good deliberation," he left a post of fifteen men on Roanoke provisioned for two years, to hold the fort. He has been criticized for a wrong decision; but we do not know his circumstances or his instructions. It looks clear to me that he was expected to reinforce the existing colony, not plant a new one, nor is it likely that his people would volunteer to make a new settlement unprepared. The real point is that Drake's unintended taking off of the colonists completely upset the planned synchronization of Raleigh's efforts and spoiled the best chance of settlement. After that everything went wrong.

In 1587 Raleigh sent out his second colony—actually it was the fourth voyage he had set forth—under John White. This had a somewhat different plan: it was not intended to supersede Roanoke but to supplement it with a settlement on the Chesapeake, and Raleigh gave White, as governor with twelve assistants, a charter to found the city of Raleigh in Virginia—a measure of self-government. Raleigh's directions were never carried out, for the sailors refused to carry the colonists to the Chesapeake and insisted on landing them on Roanoke. The colonists insisted on John White returning for further supplies, and that was the last that was ever heard of them. Some think that they perished on their way through the forest to the Chesapeake, and that is likely enough: in their fate forerunners to how many countless pioneers who perished in the American wilderness.

In the spring of 1588, Raleigh sent out a couple of small pinnaces, which never got across the Atlantic in the disturbed conditions of that memorable summer. At Bideford, Grenville was fitting out his strongest expedition yet, three tall ships and four barques. But with the Armada on the way he was not allowed to go: his Virginia voyage countermanded, he was ordered to take his ships around to Plymouth and serve under Drake. In 1589, everything in the West Country went into the big Lisbon expedition under Drake and Norris, which was England's riposte to the Armada. These years were full of work and activity for Ra-

leigh and Grenville. As Lord Lieutenant of Cornwall, Raleigh was responsible for the land defenses of the county most exposed to invasion. He was kept busy in the west, at court, and in Ireland. In 1591 Grenville was killed in the last fight of the *Revenge*, celebrated by Raleigh in unforgettable prose. The next year, with tension relaxed, Raleigh fell into utter disgrace with the Queen. Everything that he had so far been able to do was due to his favor with her: he had no independent position or footing, he was not a peer of the realm with estates and a feudal dependence, he had no fortune of his own. It all depended on his position with the Queen.

A man like Raleigh had a difficult razor-edge to walk. The Queen liked very masculine types—though they also had to be intelligent. The language in which this maiden lady delighted was the language of love: a difficult situation for these high-spirited, highly sexed men, supposed to be in love with her, though of course it was a platonic relationship, always at a certain distance. Nothing more exacting than to be admitted to so privileged an intimacy and at the same time to keep your distance and your head. For their vestal virgin who presided over it all was a jealous deity: they could have neither the Queen nor anybody else. It was more than flesh and blood could stand, particularly the hot flesh and blood of these Elizabethan courtiers. One after the other lost his balance, toppled over, and fetched up for a spell in the Tower.

Raleigh was pretty free with women; at last he fell seriously in love with one and was caught; another Elizabeth, a Throckmorton and—what made it worse—a maid of honor to the Queen. It became evident, I think, that Raleigh had, in the technical sense, behaved badly: he compromised her, or they compromised each other. To the Queen, for psychological reasons that one can understand though perhaps not wholly sympathize with, the offense was unpardonable—after such protestations of love, a passion on an altogether higher plane, for her. Raleigh made it worse by denying that he had any intention of marrying the lady. The Queen clapped them both in the Tower and had them ignominiously married, no one knows when or how. She never admitted Lady Raleigh to her presence again; for her, poor lady, it was a prelude to a lifetime of trouble. I hope that Raleigh's fine phrase when condemned to death by James—"I chose you, and I loved you, in my happiest times"—made up a little for it with her. They seem to have remained always in love; perhaps it was just as well, though

Raleigh may have had some doubts when, for the next five years, the Queen kept him away from court and all influence, in the prime of his powers.

In the last years of the Queen's reign Raleigh came back to his place at court, though things were never quite the same between them again. In 1600 he was made governor of Jersey, and local tradition there credits him with beginning the trade between the Channel Islands and Newfoundland. Raleigh was preparing to renew his contacts when James came to the throne, and Raleigh not long after was condemned for treason. He spent practically the rest of his life in the Tower; not a very good base from which to conduct colonial enterprises. However, he maintained his interest and his belief in the future of Virginia. "I shall yet live to see it an English nation," he wrote grandly from imprisonment.

How to strike a balance in estimating Raleigh's colonial achievements, his services to America? He was criticized in his own day, as he has been in ours, for not doing more. That splendid intellect but not very nice man, Francis Bacon, who was not above kicking a man when he was down, wrote in his essay "Of Plantations," "it is the sinfullest thing in the world to forsake or destitute a plantation once in forwardness, for besides the dishonour, it is the guiltiness of blood of many commiserable persons." Everyone would know whom he had in mind. But Hakluyt, who knew all the facts and was in a better position to judge, says simply that Raleigh was disheartened by the great expense and by the unfaithfulness of those he employed, "after he had sent (as you may see by these five several times) colonies and supplies at his own charges and now at length both himself and his successors [are] thus betrayed."

We have seen something, not only of his difficulties and disappointments, the obstacles in the way, but of the sheer impossibility of getting his orders executed on the other side of the Atlantic in his own enforced absence. Armchair critics of today often do not have the imagination to appreciate the physical and other conditions upon which achieving anything in the Elizabethan Age depended, how much men were at the mercy of circumstances, of wind and weather, of personal caprice or royal favor, the undependability of agents, the perversity of things.

Yet Raleigh's efforts did bear fruit: a people's mem-

Fortifications in Bermuda, here and on the following pages, as illustrated in John Smith's Generall Historie *(1624).*

ory is more generous, and perhaps speaks more truly, than the professors'. Raleigh put Virginia on the map. The first Roanoke colony was of prime formative significance; subsequent colonial enterprise in America built on that foundation. By his position at Elizabeth's court he gave the most powerful impetus in practice to the idea of English settlement in America. Even his patronage of smoking tobacco, giving it social cachet, was not without its effect in helping Virginia's staple product, the crop by which she ultimately achieved economic viability.

The approaching end of the war with Spain, at the turn of the century, made it certain that the English would now resume their efforts to settle in North America. After all, that was what they had fought Spain for—with success. The Queen would not make peace without guarantees for the Netherlands and the principle of the open door in America. On that, negotiations had broken down in 1598 and 1599. When they were renewed, after her death, Spain was in a still weaker position to insist, and peace was made in London, the negotiations dominated by Cecil, who represented the continuity of Elizabethan policy. The government obtained all that it wished in regard to the Netherlands. With regard to America, there was no agreement. The Spaniards refused to accept the English position of freedom of trade with all parts not in effective occupation: hence the continuance of "war beyond the line," *i.e.*, the Pope's line, and the subsequent romantic and bloody history of the buccaneers. On the subject of English colonization, most important of all, nothing was said. The English were not going to admit that it was a subject for discussion. The only implication to be drawn was that they would now go ahead.

Already, exploratory voyages to the coast had been resumed, and with a clear sense, expressed in the narratives, of the continuity with those of the 1580's. The French, also, now released from civil war and from war with Spain by the Treaty of Vervins (1598), took up once more their long-suspended colonial ambitions, and there followed the first settlement in Acadia, at Port Royal. In these years the great Champlain was exploring these coasts and in 1608 clinched French power in the St. Lawrence with the founding of Quebec. Already the intrepid navigator Henry Hudson was scouring the Arctic ice from Greenland to Spitsbergen to find a way through to the East, and the next year (1609) was exploring the Hudson and the Delaware river valleys on behalf of the Dutch. A new phase of international rivalry for North America was beginning.

In 1606 a body chiefly of West Countrymen came together to petition James I for license to plant a colony—Raleigh's rights having lapsed by his condemnation for treason. From this patent the subsequent colonization sprang, in the northern part of Virginia (*i.e.,* New England) as well as the south. For it constituted two companies to carry out the twin projects envisaged in north and south. The southern company was to plant between 34 and 41 degrees north, and was backed mainly from London. The northern colony was to plant between 38 and 45 degrees north; it was backed mainly from Bristol, Exeter, and Plymouth, but came to be known as the Plymouth Company. The strength of the Plymouth Company, it was hoped, would lie in its fishing interests; the London Company's in finance. Finance and fishing—there could be no doubt which would emerge the stronger. Though there was some interaction between the two, and more friction, I leave the Plymouth Company to a later article: from it sprang, if in various ways and in varying degrees, the colonization of New England.

Money and management were to be supplied by the city of London; and here the merchants weighed in, above all the East India magnate Sir Thomas Smythe, to whom the establishment and survival of the colony at Jamestown is chiefly due. It is significant that where the independent and ill co-ordinated resources of courtiers, gentlemen, and merchants had not answered earlier, the resources of the City merchants, made more maneuverable by the mechanism of the joint-stock company, succeeded. One must pay tribute to the unfaltering leadership of these merchant magnates—both Smythe and his opponent, Sir Edwin Sandys, with their supporters in the City—in all the discouragements and disasters that befell Virginia, for its ill luck continued, on the Chesapeake as at Roanoke. Lesser men would have given up in despair, would have had to for want of resources. But these men had, no less important, resource, resilience, flexibility: they turned their hands to anything rather than see it fail. And this time they saw it through.

The little fleet of three ships, the *Susan Constant, Godspeed,* and *Discovery,* with the usual complement of 100 men, sailed in December, 1606, under the command of

Pembroks forte
K

Captain Christopher Newport. Now a man of forty, who had been concerned in the capture of the *Madre de Dios,* richest of the prizes in the war, he was one of the best-esteemed sea captains of the day.

Newport brought his ships safe into the Chesapeake without let or hindrance. George Percy, brother of Raleigh's companion in the Tower—the "Wizard Earl" of Northumberland, tells us of "fair meadows and goodly tall trees, with such fresh-waters running through the woods, as I was almost ravished at the first sight thereof." They picked on the site of Jamestown, low and marshy as it was, unhealthy as it proved to be, because, being almost an island, it was defensible. There they constructed their fort. In obedience to their instructions they explored up the James River, till they were checked at the falls where now Richmond is.

We note the continuing stress upon finding a passage through to the Pacific; they were continually led to hope by stories of the Indians about a sea just beyond the mountains, and hope was not entirely extinguished until the end of the century. It is tribute to Captain John Smith's sense that he describes the bounds of Virginia as on the east "the great ocean; on the south lieth Florida; on the north Nova Francia; as for the west thereof, the limits are unknown." To discover them constituted the saga of the American people, and not until a couple of generations ago was the process, set in being by the Elizabethans, complete. In that sense, looking over the last prairie country to be settled, going through Rockies or Cascades, we may feel ourselves for a moment linked, in touch, with those first Elizabethans who started it all.

Theirs were the sacrifices; and the cost in human life in the first two decades of Virginia was terrible. No doubt this first venture was experimental and exploratory. Captain John Smith says that they had eaten up their provisions on too long a sea voyage, had arrived too late to plant, and in any case were insufficiently provided. He adds philosophically, "such actions have ever since the world's beginning been subject to such accidents, and everything of worth is found full of difficulties, but nothing so difficult as to establish a commonwealth so far remote from men and means, and where men's minds are so untoward as neither do well themselves nor suffer others." In other words, there was what is called the human factor—and it proved very human.

There is no point in entertaining illusions about it —these voyages transported the flotsam and jetsam of humanity, even the better-than-average proved selfish and listless and would not work to save themselves, let alone others. Famine and the marshes bred disease, and men began to die. Without any concentration of authority, bickerings and quarrels increased. By the end of the first winter, they were down to 38 men left alive.

Then the first supply arrived just in time, for they might have given up. (The colony planted contemporaneously by the Plymouth Company in the north at Sagadahoc did give up and went home.) With two supplies sent out in 1608 things began to look up; buildings that had been burned down were repaired, and the colonists began to plant a little. Faced with a second winter of privation, Captain John Smith,  "whom no persuasions could persuade to starve," came to the fore and as president took matters forcefully in hand. "If any would not work, neither should he eat"; he threatened to drive those who would not work into the wilderness.

By these means, and by his own energy and force of character, Smith carried the colony successfully through the second winter with few losses.

That winter the colonists had enough novelties, excitements, dangers, consolations, to last them a lifetime. They kept Christmas in bad weather, "among the savages, where we were never more merry, nor fed on more plenty of good oysters, fish, flesh, wild fowl and good bread, nor never had better fires in England than in the dry smoky houses of Kecoughtan." Relations with the Indians had all the complexity of contacts between races at very different levels of civilization, by turns friendly and hostile—or rather, the same emotions in the same breast, so that a sharp lookout had to be kept all the time. The company at home insisted on the coronation of Powhatan, the leading chief of the area, against Smith's better judgment: of "subtle understanding and politic carriage," he was rendered all the more difficult to deal with.

The most dangerous moment came when the small group of Germans in the colony conspired, characteristically, to betray it. They surreptitiously smuggled weapons to the natives and hoped to betray the colony to Spain. Equally characteristically, they got what was coming to them; a brace who got away to Powhatan had their brains beaten out for their treachery to the English. Then the Indians gave a masque, or entertainment, in the woods, after which their women pursued the embarrassed Smith with their pressing endearments. Or Powhatan's pretty daughter Pocahontas, not yet however nubile, would turn cart wheels naked in the streets of Jamestown to delight the hearts of the planters.

At home in England a wave of interest in Virginia was rising to the height of a national enterprise. The undertaking was gathering way and was launched in 1609 with the second charter, the effective instrument in the creation of Virginia. For this incorporated the Virginia Company that governed the colony and saw it through its infancy to a permanent existence, and separated it from the Plymouth Company, concerned now only with the north. The Virginia Company drew upon a most impressive array of support that can truly be said to represent the nation. It came to include 56 city companies and some 659 individuals—21 peers, 96 knights, 28 esquires, 58 gentlemen, 110 merchants, 282 citizens, and so on. To read the names of the adventurers is like hearing a roll call of the most active elements in the society of the last years of Shakespeare. There they all are, from the Archbishop of Canterbury and Shakespeare's own patrons, the Earls of Southampton, Pembroke, and Montgomery, through many names with more distant echoes, for there are Cecils and Cromwells and Chamberlains, Lord North along with the Spencer ancestor of the Churchills, while the Winston ancestor took shares later; Anglican bishops alongside of Puritans and Catholics; famous figures in the life of London down to an obscure Cornish squire like William Roscarrock, living there on the Atlantic coast near Padstow; or Gabriel and John Beadle, two poor gentlemen who went out to Virginia in the first supply (1608). Everybody who was anybody seems to have been in it, except the poets— and they as usual were short of cash.

The jealous attentions of the Spanish ambassador Zuñiga were aroused. Amazed at the response to Virginia in English society, he wrote home to Philip III that "fourteen earls and barons have given 40,000 ducats, the merchants give much more, and there is no poor little man nor woman who is not willing to subscribe something . . . Much as I have written to your Majesty of the determination they have formed here to go to Virginia, it seems to me that I still fall short of the reality."

For Virginia itself the effective change made by the second charter was the appointment of a governor with real power and authority, advised but not displaceable by the council there. The governor appointed, Lord De la Warr, was to follow Sir Thomas Gates, who meanwhile went as his deputy, with Sir George Somers as admiral of the fleet of eight ships that left Plymouth in May. This had some six hundred colonists on board, including one hundred women: the largest expedition for America until the mass emigration to Massachusetts started in 1630.

The sailing of Somers' little fleet has been described as "the true beginning of one of the great folk movements of history," but Virginia's ill luck held good. To avoid Spanish attentions and a long sea voyage, Somers' fleet took a direct course across the Atlantic from the Canaries. They ran into a hurricane, and Somers' flagship was cast away upon the coast of Bermuda, though all the folk were saved. The "still-vexed Bermoothes" were thought by the Elizabethans to be haunted by evil spirits. Out of the fusion of those two inspirations—for several accounts of it circulated at home—came *The Tempest*.

The castaways found it pleasant and healthful, with plenty to eat; and there they passed an agreeable winter, while building a couple of pinnaces to take them to Virginia. The rest of the fleet, with four hundred of the people, had arrived there in a battered condition and went through a terrible winter. This was the real "starving time" in Virginia history. By the time their leaders arrived from Bermuda in the spring, of all the four hundred and those there before, only some sixty remained alive. No doubt they brought disease with them, after so exhausting a journey, but the main reason for the disaster—it was no less—was the absence of leadership, of all authority and discipline. Elizabethans simply could not operate without it. With their leaders wrecked in Bermuda—for all they knew, drowned—the colony went to pieces.

Provisions and livestock were all consumed; the Indians refused trade except for the colonists' arms, implements, and utensils, and then turned on them, till "there remained not past sixty men, women and children, most miserable and poor creatures; and those were preserved for the most part, by roots, herbs, acorns, walnuts, berries, now and then a little fish . . ." There was, in fact, an instance or two of cannibalism.

When Gates arrived he set himself to restore order sternly; but there was little he could do; men went on dying, and there were only four days' provisions left when the colony gave up and set sail down the river. On their way they met the incoming governor, Lord De la Warr, so long delayed, and they were turned back to Jamestown. Here, under proper authority, they were set to work once more: "every man endeavoureth to outstrip other in diligence: the French preparing to plant the vines, the English labouring in the woods and grounds; every man knoweth his charge, and dischargeth the same with alacrity."

At home Sir Thomas Smythe needed every ounce of confidence to keep the adventurers to the task. In the absence of any return on their money, with repeated calls for further supplies, the discouragements of all these disasters, the persistent run of ill luck, and the rumors circulating against the colony in consequence, Smythe needed courage and statesmanship of the highest order to pull things round. These he possessed. He was a man of immense capacity and experience, of unhurried judgment and weighty decision, a somewhat impersonal man, who had the confidence of both the city and the court.

Faced with a crisis in those affairs and finding that Bermuda now looked more promising, he called in Bermuda to redress the balance of Virginia. He obtained from the Crown a third charter for Virginia, extending her bounds 300 leagues from the continent to include Bermuda. A Bermuda, or Somers Islands, company was floated on a joint-stock, began to make profits from an immense piece of ambergris found on the coast, and started to colonize.

The new charter permitted a lottery to be started, with prizes, to raise cash. And later the company became chiefly a land company, "its one asset the land that had been bought with the sacrifices of the first ten years." The company appealed to intending planters with an offer of fifty acres for every person to be sent to the colony; on this basis plantation continued and was extended—whatever the setbacks now, settlement went on.

Within the colony, too, the corner may be said to have been turned with the change from communal arrangements to private ownership. No doubt the first tasks in a new settlement were communal in their nature. But when the soldier-governors allotted every man in the settlement three acres of clear ground to his own, they turned from bowling in the street to cultivating their gardens. Progress was at once to be seen. At the same time, what was to become Virginia's staple export, tobacco, makes its first appearance. The credit for the first experiments is thought to be John Rolfe's. He made another experiment, too, which has brought him greater fame: he fell in love with Pocahontas, and she with him. After much deliberation with his friends, and some prayer, he married her properly. This favorably impressed the Indians, and for some years there was a blissful interval of peace and good relations.

Rolfe later brought Pocahontas to England, where she "unexpectedly" died—of the climate, perhaps.

Now that the colony had been brought round, the man by whose efforts it had been accomplished, Sir Thomas Smythe, lost control of the Virginia Company and received his dismissal, in the usual way of such things. There always had been a division in the company between the big City merchants and the more numerous small adventurers, between the platform and the floor of the house. (As usual, the platform was generally right, the floor generally wrong.) Again, as usual, the discontented majority found leadership among the magnates: in the Earl of Warwick, in Shakespeare's Southampton, and above all in Sir Edwin Sandys.

Sandys, who became treasurer of the company in 1619, was a remarkable man. Educated under Richard Hooker at Oxford, where he became a Fellow of Corpus Christi College, he was much more of an intellectual than Sir Thomas Smythe. He toured Europe with Archbishop Cranmer's great nephew and dedicated the book he wrote, *Europae speculum,* to Archbishop Whitgift. We see that his early associations were archiepiscopal. This did not prevent him from being rather a demagogue in the House of Commons, where he was very forward in opposition.

In the Virginia Company Sandys captured the leadership of the lesser shareholders, many of whom, including fifty Members of Parliament, had not paid up their subscriptions. Sandys thereupon resorted to lotteries; he was very ingenious and resourceful, full of energy and ideas, up to anything and everything to raise money. And we must do him this justice: he did infuse new energy into, gave a fresh impetus to, the colony. After his first year of office, James refused to have him renominated: "Choose the Devil, if you will, but not Sir Edwin Sandys." So Southampton was elected treasurer, though Sandys remained the moving spirit.

Sir Edwin, I fear, was a sharp customer. When it came to depressing reports from Virginia, he and John and Nicholas Ferrars doctored the minutes. An adept at maneuvering votes in council, by 1622 he had got into control of both companies. He now proposed a scheme of salaries for himself and offices for his supporters that was unprecedented. He as director was to receive £500 a year. Smythe, after five years as governor of the East India Company, had refused to accept more than £400 gratuity. For twelve years' service as treasurer of the Virginia Company he was rewarded with twenty shares; Sandys got as much for one year, and John Ferrars as his deputy, the same amount for three years. It is not the first time that a reformer has been revealed as self-interested.

Meanwhile, so engrossed were they in these characteristic amenities of committees, idiotic dissensions, and personal maneuvers that the terrible Indian massacre of that year—in which 350 were killed and 500

more died within the twelvemonth—went unnoticed, so far as remedies went. Sandys and the Ferrarses suppressed information as to the worst miseries the colony endured, and put about misleading reports. But disquiet about Virginia grew, and Smythe's governor, back from Bermuda, revealed the facts of Sandys' feverish overshipping of colonists and the fearful mortality in consequence. He had certainly been energetic. In the four years of Sandys' administration 4,000 had been transported; the net increase to the population was 275. In all, by 1622 some 10,000 souls had gone out to Virginia; of these only 2,000 were alive. As to money, under Smythe £80,000 had been expended; in the far shorter period of Sandys, between £80,000 and £90,000.

No: the effective founder of Jamestown colony was Sir Thomas Smythe.

These facts were revealed by a committee appointed by the Crown, which exonerated Smythe's administration, going through all the books and figures, and condemned Sandys. There was furious dissension, for of course Sandys retained the support of the Commons. But the government had had enough of it; when Sandys and his allies appealed to the Commons, the Crown recalled the Virginia charters and resumed the government of the colony into its own hands: henceforth this took the classic shape of royal governors with assistants nominated by the Crown, with a representative assembly.

We may take this to end the founding phase in the colony's history. Up to 1624 the whole cost of the plantation of Virginia was about £200,000, with what little return we have seen. We may profitably contrast the money poured out by England to settle her stock in Virginia with Spain's ruthless exploitation of the West Indies—the regular drain of treasure from Mexico and Peru.

Within the colony, after such tribulations, all was at last set fair. Even before the last of them, the Indian Massacre of 1622, a most important development in government took place, from which the ultimate form of American government was shaped: the first representative assembly, based on popular election, met there in the tiny church beside the river at Jamestown. A touching scene in its simplicity and yet in all that it signifies—the heart of the political experience of the English-speaking peoples and the peculiar contribution they have to make to the world.

At home the interest displayed in very different quarters tells its own story. In matters of policy James I did not depart from the stand Queen Elizabeth had taken on America, though there were people, Sir Edwin Sandys among them, who were afraid that he might give way to the Spaniards. Anyway, in the first years that mattered most, he had Cecil beside him to guide policy on the Elizabethan lines. James's own interest did not amount to much. We have an exchange between Southampton and Salisbury in 1609 which shows what they thought. James had heard of the Virginia squirrels that were said to fly, and asked Southampton whether there were none for him, and whether Salisbury had not provided some for him. Southampton would not have told Salisbury, "but that you know so well how he is affected to these toys." One notices the contrast between the lightheaded James in these matters and the profound and tenacious concern of the great Queen. And indeed nothing could have advertised that contrast more signally to the world than James's execution of Raleigh at the behest of Spain.

More worthy of respect is the interest of ordinary Englishmen in all walks of life in the new England rising on the other side of the Atlantic. The bishops raised a fund of some £2,000 for an Indian college and for the support of an Indian school, though the company was too short of funds to use them for the purpose. One day in November, 1620, a stranger stepped into a meeting of the court and presented Raleigh's history of Guiana, with a map and four great books, for the college; twelve months later a stranger again came forward with more books for the college. Most touching of all are the collections made on board the East Indiamen for Virginia. In 1621 at the Cape of Good Hope, the *Royal James* collected £70 6s. 8d. toward building a free school, the highest amount ten marks from Captain Pring, and so down to 1 shilling from the mariners. Two other ships collected 100 marks—in all £192 1s. 10d.—that Virginia might have a school. When we think of the hard conditions of those sailors' lives, and out of their little pay contributing their shillings, we glimpse something of what America meant for those simple English folk.

On the other hand, there is all that the old country meant for the new. Professor Wesley Frank Craven rightly emphasizes that the beginnings of American history can properly be read only forward from the Elizabethan England of which it was an extrapolation, not backwards from modern America. He is writing in particular about the South, though what he says also applies with little change to the North:

The historian who would trace the main threads woven into the pattern of Southern life must, therefore, turn first to England. . . . For it was the Elizabethan Englishman who planned and undertook the settlements to which most of us look back as on our beginnings. The Elizabethan tongue that once rang out across the James and the York may still be heard in certain out-of-the-way spots of the South. The Elizabethan devotion to Protestantism, born of a long defense of Elizabeth's church settlement and fed on the fiery materials of John Foxe's *Book of Martyrs*, still survives to shape the fundamental tenets of the great majority of Southerners. Even the institutional pattern our forefathers adapted to the peculiar requirements of a new-world environment was more Elizabethan than anything else. Though sheriffs, coroners, constables, justices of the peace, juries, and representative assemblies were ancient parts of the English scene, it was as their place and function had been defined under Elizabeth that the early colonists understood them. Here, too, has the South, ever prompt to recognize individual achievement, discovered the first heroic figures of her history—Elizabeth herself and Raleigh.

This is the second part of a series specially prepared for AMERICAN HERITAGE *by Dr. A. L. Rowse, Fellow of All Souls College, Oxford, and noted authority on the Elizabethan era. In the third, which will appear in August, Dr. Rowse turns to New England, Sir Ferdinando Gorges, and the little-known voyages that preceded the Plymouth Colony.*

☆ ☆ ☆ ☆ ☆ ☆ ☆ ☆ ☆ ☆ ☆

One of the most striking characteristics of an American is his self dependence. Born to no fortune, he knows from his earliest years that he has nothing but his own mental and bodily exertions to rely on in the great struggle of existence. This self dependence produces a remarkable quickness and versatility of talent. He turns his mother wit, as the Indian does his knife, to all purposes, and is seldom at a loss. At his first outset in life the world lies before him, like the wilderness of his own country, a trackless waste through which he must cut his own path; but what would be a region of doubt and despondency to another mind appears to him a land of promise, a region of glorious enterprize tinted with golden hope.

—*From an unpublished essay by Washington Irving, 1831; courtesy of Mary A. Benjamin, Director, Walter R. Benjamin Autographs.*

"*Charlie, your son is a genius . . .*"

*The cutouts reproduced on this page are the work of a gifted child of eight. His name was Charles Dana Gibson, and he grew up to become the illustrator who created that famous turn-of-the-century symbol, the Gibson Girl (*AMERICAN HERITAGE, *December, 1957). According to his sister, Mrs. Josephine Gibson Knowlton, in her reminiscence,* Longfield, *young Gibson's family at first seemed to take his ability with a scissors for granted; in fact, the cutout at bottom right would indicate that it was even somewhat of a nuisance. "Please, Master Dana," his nurse begs, "no more paper on the floor." Then one day the boy's great-uncle took his father aside. "Charlie," he said, displaying a bunch of the cutouts, "your son is a genius. Your Dana is a boy of eight, and can bring to life on paper anything he sees just once. . . . Mark my word, you have a son who will give a new meaning to the word 'artist'."*